Glossary of Hausa Music
and Its Social Contexts

Glossary of Hausa Music
and Its Social Contexts

David W. Ames
and
Anthony V. King

Northwestern University Press
Evanston   1971

David W. Ames is an anthropologist at San Francisco State College.
Anthony V. King is an ethnomusicologist at the School of Oriental
and African Studies, University of London.

All photographs in this book were taken by the authors.

Contents

205145

Introduction

The richness, variety and complexity of the cultures
of the Hausa city-states are illustrated in microcosm in
this work, in which over one-hundred terms for musical instruments were collected for the kingdoms of Zaria and
Katsina alone; and, no doubt, more will be identified in
subsequent investigations. Complexity was encountered in
other aspects of musical life, e.g., in the manifold
classes of professional musicians, reflecting an extraor-
dinary range of specialization in musical performance. As
this suggests, the authors -- one an anthropologist and
the other a musicologist -- have attempted to make this
more than a technical glossary of musical instruments and
sound production; in fact, it has grown to be a kind of
shorthand ethnography of musical life, in which equal
weight is given to the socio-cultural context of musical
performance, as well.

Scope

Limiting the glossary to realistic proportions involves the problem of definition of the geographical, cultural and linguistic context for data collection. The
Hausa language is spoken by more persons in sub-Saharan
Africa than any other African language, and, obviously,
the geographical distribution of its speakers is not nec-

essarily coterminous with the bearers of what might be loosely termed Hausa culture. Hausa recognition of a cultural dichotomy between the Hausa bakwai ("Hausa Seven," i.e., the seven authentic Hausa states) and the banza bakwai ("Worthless Seven," i.e., the seven impostor states) could serve as a valid basis for the limitation of data collection were it currently possible to define the boundaries of those states most popularly described as the Hausa bakwai; unfortunately, the nineteenth century jihad of Usuman 'Dan Fodiyo effected not only a change of social organization within the traditional geographic boundaries of the Hausa bakwai, but it also effected the removal of considerable population elements of these Ha'be (original Hausa) states to new geographical areas and the development of new cultural contexts.

We are thus forced either to attempt coverage of the whole of present-day Hausaland (involving extremely invidious cultural distinctions and an unrealistically large collection area) or to attempt an arbitrary selection of area or areas. Assuming this latter course to be the more practicable, it would then be advisable to choose areas coterminous with, and showing the closest social and cultural derivation from, the pre-jihad states. We are thus left with the present-day emirates of Kano, Katsina, Zaria, and Daura.

For this work, the authors have focused on two of

these administrative and cultural areas, Katsina and
Zaria, not because they are more important than the others
but simply because most of the authors' field work was
done there. (Note: Ames carried out an anthropological
study of the status and role of Hausa musicians in Zaria
in 1963-64 and King carried out his ethno-musicological
investigations in Katsina in 1963-65 and in 1968.) Data
from other areas are occasionally included if they are
historically noteworthy, e.g., in the case of the royal
drums (tambura) of the Ha'be kingdoms of Daura and Abuja.

Not surprisingly, we found that the Hausa had no
equivalents for some Western definitions, and vice versa.
For example, the Hausa do not have a popular term for "music". Use of the term musika (? Arabic derivation) is
confined to an extremely limited number of malamai (sing.,
malan; a Koranic scholar). Terms such as bushe-bushe
(sing., busa; blowing), ka'de-ka'de (sing., ki'da; beating, shaking, plucking, or bowing), and wak'e-wak'e
(sing., wak'a; singing), although describing the various
methods of producing music, refer basically to performance
technique rather than to the actual organization of sonorities. Similarly derived nouns of agent, e.g., mabusa
(sing., mabushi), maka'da (sing., maka'di), and mawak'a
(sing., mawak'i), refer to the performer's instrument in
distinguishing between classes of musicians. The nearest
equivalent to a popular generic term for "music" is rok'o

(begging), but this term neither covers all organization
of sonorities (e.g., it does not include amateur music-
making) nor strictly excludes non-musical activities; it
is, in effect, a reflection of social attitudes towards
the musician rather than towards his product.

Account will be taken in this work not only of words
referring to actual organizations of sonorities, but also
of those referring to the social and ideational contexts
and contents of such organizations. We have unavoidably
resorted to the use of some Western categories for section
headings; however, whenever possible, we have used Hausa
categories to illustrate their cognitive system, as in the
case of major classes of performers and generic terms for
certain classes of instruments -- for example, <u>ganga</u>, a
large class of double membrane drums.

Finally, it should be stressed that we do not hold
this to be a definitive work. Indeed it is only a beginning or a statement of how far we have progressed with our
study in this largely uncharted area.

Presentation of Material

The glossary is a Hausa-English collection, i.e.,
terms will be listed alphabetically under their Hausa
form. Although this is the only practicable way to present such material, difficulties of use for non-Hausa
speakers can be overcome with the help of the English-

Hausa Index and the alphabetized index of Hausa terms.
The reader is also advised to consult the introduction of
each section for definitions and explanations of the numerical and letter indices.

Where understanding of the meaning of a term can be
supplemented by demonstration of its use within the language, we have done so, and especially where the use of a
term is an accepted form of expression (e.g., proverb,
riddle, praise, etc.), throwing light on its social value.
Where a term applies to some aspect of the organization of
sonorities, examples will be scientifically described as
far as possible.

Orthography

The standard orthography as used by the Gaskiya Corporation (printers to the Government of Northern Nigeria)
is utilized as far as possible, with the following excep-
tions which are due to the printing process used in this
work: the implosive voiced consonants will be written
'b and 'd and the plosive with a glottal stop (ejective)
will be written k' as in G.P. Bargery's Hausa-English Dictionary (Oxford University Press, 1957). Although Hausa
speakers have no difficulty with the Gaskiya Corporation
orthography, non-Hausa speakers may wish to consult R.C.
Abraham's Dictionary of the Hausa Language (University of
London Press, 1962) for additional phonemic information.

Acknowledgements

Ames' research was assisted by grants awarded by the Joint Committee on African Studies of the Social Science Research Council and the American Council of Learned Societies and the Faculty Research Committee of San Francisco State College. King's field research was carried out while at the University of Ibadan on an appointment financed by a grant from the Ford Foundation of America to that institution, and in 1968 a second period of research was assisted by a grant from the Nuffield Foundation and the Central Research Fund of the University of London.

The authors are especially indebted to Barbara Ames for spending many many hours preparing and editing the manuscript for this work.

The authors also wish to express their gratitude to the following persons and institutions for assisting them at various stages of their work: Alhaji Muhammadu Aminu, Emir of Zaria; Alhaji Sir Usuman Nagogo, C.N.Q., Emir of Katsina; the late Alhaji Muhammadu Sanusi, Waziri of Zaria; Alhaji Hasan Rafindadi, Sarkin Yak'i of Katsina; Malan Ibrahim Bagudu, Madauci of Zaria; Malan Muhammadu Bello; Malan Kontagora Salisu Ahmed; Malan Salisu Kontagora; Malan Aminu Yero; Malan Isaac Umar; Malan Dauda Bagari; Malan Mohammed 'Danbala; Malan Bello Daura; Malan Rashid Ibrahim; Malan Kabir M. Galadanci; Malan Abbas Meslin; Malan Ibrahim Mukoshey; David W. Arnott;

M. Hiskett; A.H.M. Kirk-Greene; Alan Merriam; J.P.S. Montagu; M.G. Smith; the Institute of African Studies of Ibadan University; and the Institute of Administration of Ahmadu Bello University.

Glossary of Hausa Music and Its Social Contexts

I. Instruments
and Their Parts

Notes on Numerical and Letter Indices

In the lists of instruments that follow --

Numerical indices in the right-hand margin are those of the Sachs-Hornbostel Classification; supplementary letter indices thereunder are used as follows:

o. - performer with official status;

no. - performer without official status;

p. - performer of professional status;

np. - performer of non-professional status.

Information, where available, is presented in the following order:

1. General physical description and average dimensions where critical.

2. Terms for parts of the instrument and materials of construction.

3. Performance technique.

4. Ensemble combinations.

5. Social usage.

6. References in oral "literature" indicative of social values attaching to an instrument, its performer, or its performance, such references being drawn from _kirari_ (traditional identificatory texts, often of an epithetical form) and _karin_ _magana_ (proverbial sayings).

1) Idiophones

acikoko m.s.   112.13
                                                                   no.np.

1. Pair of globular seed-pods partially filled with
   small stones, seeds, or other materials, and joined
   together by a short length of string and used as a
   rattle.

3. One pod is held in the palm of the hand and the other swung so that the string loops the hand and the
   second "free" pod strikes the first periodically.

4. Used in the accompaniment of song.

5. Used by young people of either sex for informal
   music-making.

agidigo m.s. (d.f. Yoruba, agidigbo)   122.12
= jita m.s. (d.f. English, guitar)   no.p.

1. Plucked idiophone constructed from a number of metal
   lamellae mounted on a wooden box-resonator.

3. Positioned on lap or suspended from neck in a horizontal position at waist level, so that the lamellae
   may be plucked with the fingers of either hand.

4. Used solo or in combination with kalangu, 'dan
   kar'bi and kuntuku in the accompaniment of song.

5. Used by musicians known as karen gusau for entertainment songs (wak'ar nasha'di) or, prior to January, 1966, for political songs (wak'ar siyasa).

bambaro m.s.   121.221
                                                                   no.np.

1. Iron Jew's (jaw's) harp of local manufacture.

3. Held by the left hand between the open lips and
   teeth of the mouth, the lamella being plucked either
   towards or away from the face by the player's right
   hand; simultaneous tongue and glottal movement

effect harmonic alterations, thus permitting the imitation of the syllable tones and vowel qualities of an underlying language text.

4. Used as a solo instrument.

5. Used by young people of either sex for informal music-making.

---

barancaki m.s. (pl. barancakai)   112.13
= barankaci m.s. (pl. barankatai)   no.np.

1. Long flatish dried seed pod of the barancaki plant, used as a hand-held rattle.

3. Held at its end in the right hand and beaten against the open palm of the left hand.

4. Used solo or in combination with other barancakai in the accompaniment of song.

5. Used by young people of either sex for informal music-making.

---

caccakai pl. = akacau pl.   112.121
= akayau pl. = k'oroso pl.   no.np.

1. Iron ankle rattle.

3. Tied to dancer's ankle or ankles and sounded by leg movements in dance.

5. Worn by men in such dances as rawan Gane.

---

caki m.s. = buta f.s. = duma f.s.   112.13
= galura f.s. = garura f.s.   no.p.
= gora f.s. = gyan'dama f.s.

1. Hand-held rattle from a suitable container partially filled with small stones, seeds or other suitable objects. Strictly speaking, the name of the instrument derives from the nature of the container (see under 2 below), the term caki being generic for any

instrument of this class.

2. (i) buta f.s.: a bottle-shaped gourd or tin container used for rattle body.

   (ii) duma f.s.: the generic name for any one of a
number of differently shaped gourds, in this
case the name for any bottle-shaped gourd used
for the rattle body.

   (iii) galura f.s. = garura f.s.: a bottle-shaped
gourd, used for rattle body.

   (iv) gora f.s.: a bottle-shaped gourd used for rattle body.

   (v) gyan'dama f.s.: a bottle-shaped gourd used for
rattle body.

3. Held in the right hand and shaken and beaten against
the open palm of the left hand.

4. Used either solo to accompany song or speech, solo
or with one or more other caki to accompany garaya,
komo or molo, or with garaya, komo or molo in the
joint accompaniment of song.

5. Used solo to accompany song or speech by musicians
such as 'yan garura; for ensemble combinations with
other instruments, see garaya, komo and molo.

cakansami m.s. (pl. cakansamai)   112.13
= cikansami m.s. (pl. cikansamai)   no.np.

1. Ankle rattle made from woven palm leaves and consisting of a number of small pouches partially filled with small stones, seeds, or other suitable objects.

3. Tied to dancer's ankle or ankles and sounded by leg
movements in dance.

4. Used in dancing and singing to kwairama, gangar noma
and kazagi.

5. Worn by young men and boys in such dances as rawan
Gane.

kacikaura f.s. = kacakaura f.s.   112.112
= kacaura f.s. = cakaura f.s.   no.p.
= lalajo m.s.

1. Sistrum made from a number of gourd discs strung on
   a thin straight stick, or from a number of tin discs
   strung on a short length of straight wire.

3. The ends of the stick or wire held in both hands and
   the whole shaken from side to side periodically.

4. Used solo or with one or more other kacikaura in the
   accompaniment of song.

5. Used by musicians known as 'yan kacikaura.

kasam'bara f.s. = sam'bara f.s.   131
= sham'bara f.s.   no.p.

1. A length of guinea-corn stalk with a node at one
   end, shredded lengthwise from the latter to the open
   end to form a brush-like instrument.

3. Held between the palms of the hands and rotated by
   the rubbing motion of the latter.

4. Used on its own or with one or more other kasam'bara
   in the accompaniment of garaya, or with garaya in
   the joint accompaniment of song.

5. Most frequently found in the performance of music
   for bori.

kuge m.s.   111.242.121
                                                   o.np.

1. Pair of clapperless iron, bronze or silver bells,
   joined at their apexes to the opposite sides of a
   common handle so that the larger and lower-pitched
   bell lies slightly further from the end of the handle than the other.

3. Held by the left hand in an upright position at a-
   bout shoulder level with the larger bell on the
   player's right; beaten on either bell with the
   pointed end of a duiker horn, the two pitch levels

obtainable (at an interval of approx. 220 cents)
used in the realization of the speech tones of an
organizing language text (take).

4. Used solo for proclamations, such as the announce-
ment of war, or in combination with kakakai (kakaki)
and gangar fada (ganga) in the performance of take.

5. Ownership vested in the office of Emir or in that of
one of his most senior officials (in Katsina,
K'aura; in Zaria, Madaki or Galadima), for whom it
is traditionally beaten. See masu kuge, marok'an
Sarki, sarakuna, and marok'an sarakuna.

6.a. Kirarin K'auran Katsina (kirari for K'aura of
Katsina):

Goje a kira ka da kuge
"Goje (the usual epithet for K'aura), you are
summoned with kuge!"

b. Kirarin Madakin Zazzau (Zaria):

Mai kugen tama mai kugen azurfa
"Owner of the iron kuge, owner of the silver kuge"

k'warya f.s. (pl. k'ore)   111.24
                                                          no.p.

1. Hemispherical shell of a dried half-gourd, the various sizes encountered being related to their performance usages (see under 3 below).

3. The various sizes and usages and, in some cases,
more specific terms for k'warya are:

3.1. k'warya f.s.: a small gourd inverted against the
chest and beaten with the fingers of both hands,
with or without rings thereon; used by men or wom-
en in the accompaniment of song, either singly or
with one or more other k'ore.

3.2. k'waryar kukuma f.s. ("the k'warya for kukuma"):
similar to 3.1 above, but may alternatively be
beaten with a pair of sticks; used by men or women
in the accompaniment of kukuma, or with kukuma in
the joint accompaniment of song.

3.3. k'warya f.s.: a medium or large gourd inverted on
the ground and beaten with the fingers of both
hands, with or without rings thereon; used by

women in the accompaniment of song (ki'dan amada, wak'ar bori) either singly or with one or more other k'ore.

3.4. k'waryar goge f.s. ("the k'warya for goge"): a large gourd inverted on the ground and beaten with a pair of sticks; used by men in the accompaniment of goge or with goge in the joint accompaniment of song.

3.5. k'waryar ki'dan ruwa f.s. ("the k'warya for beating on water"): the term for a member of a set of three half-gourds used by women in the accompaniment of song (ki'dan amada, wak'ar kishiya), the specific instruments being:

3.5.1. masakin ka'dawa m.s. ("the large gourd for beating") = ganga, m. or f.s. = masakin amada m.s. ("the large gourd for amada music"): a large gourd inverted on a blanket folded on the ground, and beaten with the fingers of both hands, with or without rings thereon.

3.5.2. tulluwa f.s. = tilli m.s.: a small gourd inverted and floated in a bowl of water and beaten with a small stick.

3.5.3. kazagin amada m.s. ("the kazagi for amada music") = kazagi m.s.: a small gourd inverted on the ground and beaten with a pair of sticks.

ruwan gatari m.s.   111.1
("a handleless axe-head")   no.np.

1. An iron axe-head.

3. Held in one hand and beaten against a hoe-blade (ruwan patenya) held in the other hand.

4. Used solo or with one or more other pairs of such instruments in the accompaniment of song and/or dancing.

5. Used by 'yan daji during tashe.

ruwan patenya m.s.   111.1
                                                                no.np.

1. See ruwan gatari.

sambani m.s.   111.14
                                                                no.np.

1. Two pairs of iron hand-clappers, each member of each
   pair being in the shape of a large langue du chat
   with small iron rings set into holes around the
   edge.

3. One pair is held in each hand with the second,
   third and fourth fingers supporting the upper clap-
   per, and the thumb the lower; the clappers are sepa-
   rated and brought together periodically.

4. Used solo in the accompaniment of song.

5. Used by women for the accompaniment of songs, usually on a religious topic on occasions such as weddings or naming ceremonies, for malamai on the eve
   of Mauludu, for sarakuna on the two major festivals
   of Babbar Salla and K'aramar Salla and on eclipses
   of the sun.

shantu m.s. (pl. shantuna)   111.231
                                                               no.np./p.

1. The tubular shell of a long, narrow gourd, open at
   both ends; often decorated with patterns burned on,
   or cut into, the outside shell.

3. Held in the right hand and beaten in a variety of
   ways by the seated player, including the following:

3.1. Stamped with its lower end against the inside of
     the right thigh, or against the calf of the right
     leg.

3.2. Stamped with its upper end against the open palm
     of the left hand.

3.3. Tapped with its outer shell against the shin bone
     of the right leg.

3.4. Tapped with the lip of its lower end against the ground.

3.5. Tapped on its outer shell with rings on the fingers of the right or left hand.

4. Used singly or with one or more other shantuna in the statement of zambo, as in wak'ar kishiya, karin magana (proverbial sayings), etc., through the imitation of speech tone and quantity; used solo or with one or more other shantuna in the accompaniment of song.

5. Used by women for social comment (e.g. by a co-wife in criticism of her partners) or for informal music-making. Played by a male professional singer from Kano in accompaniment of song -- but this is an exceptional case.

tandu m.s. (pl. tanduna)   111.24
                                            no.p.

1. A narrow-necked leather flask.

2.a. kan tandu m.s.: the base of the flask.

3. Held in a near-horizontal position on the left side of the body, with the base to the front, and beaten with a (right) hand-held stick and the fingers of the left hand, with or without rings thereon. Also may be beaten with hands only.

4. Used solo or with one or more other tanduna and drums in the accompaniment of humorous songs.

5. Used by a male entertainer ('yan tandu) while dancing and in the accompaniment of song.

turmi m.s. (pl. turame)   111.24
                                            no.np.

1. Large wooden mortar of the kind used for pounding cereals.

2.a. ta'barya f.s. (pl. ta'bare): pestle.

3. Rhythmic pounding of foodstuffs performed by up to three women using one pestle each. Extra percussive

effects are produced by the pestle's being struck a-
gainst the side of the <u>turmi</u> on the upstroke, followed by throwing the pestle upwards, clapping the
freed hands, and catching the pestle for the down-
stroke.

4. Pounding with up to three pestles and often used as
an accompaniment to song.

5. Used musically on such occasions as <u>lugude</u>.

<u>zari</u> m.s. 111.1

no.p.

1. Pair of iron rings.

3. Held one in each hand and beaten together.

4. Used solo or with one or more other <u>zari</u> in the accompaniment of song.

<u>zunguru</u> m.s. (pl. <u>zungura</u>) 111.231

no.p.

1. The tubular shell of a long, narrow gourd, larger
than <u>shantu</u>, with one end closed and with small iron
rings fitted around the rim of the open end.

3. Held in the hands and shaken and stamped on the
ground.

4. Used solo or with one or more other <u>zungura</u> in the
accompaniment of song.

5. Used by men and women for performances such as
<u>ki'dan</u> <u>malamai</u>.

2) <u>Membranophones</u>

<u>badujala</u> f.s. 211.212.1

no.np.

1. Imported military side-drum.

3. Normal band technique.

4. Normal band combinations.

5. Normal band usage.

bandiri m.s.
211.311
211.11
no.np.

1. Set of two or more drums, comprising the following:

1.1. Single-membrane circular frame-drum, with or without circular metal jingles.

1.2. Single-membrane bowl-shaped drum.

3.1. Frame drum held at the edge by the left hand, with the fingers positioned to mute the membrane, and beaten with the fingers of the right hand.

3.2. Bowl-shaped drum placed vertically between the folded legs and beaten with the fingers of either hand.

4. Used individually or as a set in the accompaniment or in the recitation of zikiri.

5. Used by some members of the K'adiriyya sect in the accompaniment of zikiri. Its comparatively recent introduction into the religious worship of this sect in Nigeria is attributed to Alhaji Nasiru Kabara, present-day head of the K'adiriyya; justification for its use in worship is claimed from the behaviour of Sidi Abdulkadiri, grandson of the Prophet, who performed zikiri to the accompaniment of hand-clapping.

banga m. or f.s. (pl. banguna)
211.11-852
o.p.

1. Small single-membrane bowl-shaped drum with or without a layer of wax on the membrane centre.

2.a. awara f.s.: iron lacing-ring around the base of the body.

   b. banga m. or f.s.: wooden body-shell, carved from alilliba, katsari, or k'irya trees.

    c. fata f.s.: membrane from gazelle or duiker skins.

    d. kafar zuba mai f.s.: hole in side of body-shell for pouring mixture of oil and spice therein.

    e. kirinya f.s.: hide ring lapping the membrane.

    f. k'ofar zuba mai f.s. = kafar zuba mai (supra).

    g. liko m.s.: plug for kafar zuba mai (supra).

    h. ma'dauki m.s.: cloth carrying-strap, attached to body of banga.

    i. maratayi m.s. = ma'dauki (supra).

    j. nake m.s.: wax layer on membrane centre.

    k. nike m.s. = nake (supra).

    l. rici m.s.: membrane lacing-thongs attached at their lower end to awara (supra).

    m. rigar banga f.s. ("the gown of banga") cloth bag completely covering the drum-body but leaving the membrane exposed.

3. Hung suspended from the left shoulder so that it lies at waist level in a near-vertical position slightly to the left of the body; the player, normally seated in a cross-legged position, strikes the membrane with the fingers of either hand, on or off the central wax layer.

4. Used with one or more other banguna in the accompaniment of song by the drummers themselves.

5. Used by musicians of officialdom in Zaria and Katsina in the accompaniment of songs of praise of their patron. See masu banga, Magajin Banga, marok'an Sarki, marok'an sarakuna.

'dan kar'bi m.s.   211.242.1-812
                                      o./no.p.

1. Double-membrane hourglass drum, similar to but smaller than kalangu, with which it is customarily combined. Length of body-shell - 9"; diameter of ends - 5.75"; diameter of waist - 2.375".

2. As for kalangu.

3. See kalangu.

4. See kalangu.

5. See kalangu.

duma m.s. (pl. dumamai)   2x211.221.2-852
                                                 no.p.

1. Set of two single-membrane barrel-shaped drums with
   closed ends, comprising:

1.1. duma m.s.: large gourd-bodied drum with two iron
     jingles attached. Length of body-shell - 26.5";
     diameter of open end - 10".

1.2. talle m.s.: slightly smaller gourd-bodied drum
     with one iron jingle attached. Length of body-
     shell - 25"; diameter of open end - 8".

2. Both instruments:

   a. duma m.s.: gourd body-shell.

   b. fata f.s.: membrane from goat's skin.

3. Performance technique derives to some extent from
   social usage, the two main methods of beating duma
   being:

3.1. The drums stand vertically on the ground supported
     by the knees of the seated player, with duma on
     the right-hand side and talle on the left; duma is
     beaten with a (right) hand-held stick and talle
     either with the same stick or with the fingers of
     the left hand.

3.2. Of the two drums, duma alone may be carried sus-
     pended from the left shoulder in a near-horizontal
     position under the left arm, with the membrane to
     the front; in this position it is beaten either
     with the right-hand stick or with the fingers of
     the left hand.

4. Used as a set in combination with kurya and kazagi
   for the accompaniment of song and/or dancing, the
   performance technique being as in 3.1 above. In addition duma may be used alone in combination with

kurya and kazagi for the accompaniment of processional songs and/or dancing, the performance technique being as in 3.2 above.

5. Used by men (masu duma) at aure (marriage ceremonies, including the processional escorting of the
bride), suna (naming ceremonies), and on festival
days such as Babbar Salla and K'aramar Salla.

6.a. kirarin duma:

> An ce gangana na duma ce to kowane ne a duma aka
> wanke shi
> "Though it is said my drum is only made of gourd,
> whoever a man may be, he is first washed in such
> a gourd."

duman girke m.s.   2x211.221.2-852
                                                    no.p.

1. Set of two single-membrane barrel-shaped drums with
closed ends, comprising:

1.1. duma m.s.: large wooden-bodied drum. Length of
body-shell - 27"; diameter of open end - 12".

1.2. dumanya f.s.: slightly smaller wooden-bodied
drum. Length of body-shell - 23.5"; diameter of
open end - 11".

2. As for duma, from which they are said to derive, the
main difference being in the wooden body-shells of
duman girke carved from the k'irya tree.

3. Performance technique is largely the same as for
duma, the main difference being that when the drums
stand on the ground, they do so with their bases
supported on cloth pads and without need of further
support from the player's knees.

4. As for duma.

5. See masu duma.

dundufa f.s. = dodara f.s.   211.211.2-851
= dumfa f.s. = totara f.s.   2x211.211.2-852
= tudara f.s.   no.p.

1. Set of two or three single-membrane cylindrical
   drums with closed ends. In Katsina, the set com-
   prises 1.11, 1.12, and 1.13 below, in Zaria, 1.21
   and 1.22:

1.11. uwar gida f.s. ("the senior wife"): length of
      body-shell - 36"; diameter of open end - 10".

1.12. duma m.s.: length of body-shell - 35"; diameter
      of open end - 8".

1.13. magu'diya f.s. ("the ululator"): length of body-
      shell - 33.5"; diameter of open end - 7.5".

1.21. dundufa f.s. = uwa f.s. ("the mother").

1.22. 'yar dundufa f.s. ("the daughter of dundufa").

2. All instruments:

   a. cinki m.s. = tsinke m.s.: large iron needle used
      in lacing on a new membrane, and normally kept at-
      tached to the side of magu'diya.

   b. fata f.s. = fatar akwiya f.s. = fatar tayin dalo
      f.s.: membrane of goat's skin (fatar akwiya) or
      from the foetus of a newly-born calf (fatar tayin
      dalo).

   c. furya f.s. = kwango m.s.: wooden body-shell carv-
      ed from kirya, alulluba or kawo trees.

   d. hurya f.s. = maka'di m.s.: beating stick from
      aduwa, geza or sabara trees.

   e. ido m.s. = k'ofa f.s.: hole in the side of the
      body-shell for pouring a mixture of oil and spice
      therein.

   f. kirinya f.s.: hide-ring lapping the membrane.

   g. man gya'da m.s.: ground-nut oil, poured with
      spices into the body-shell.

   h. rik'i m.s.: leather or iron lacing-ring around
      the base of the body-shell.

    i. <u>tambari</u> m.s.: calf-skin covering closed end of body-shell.

    j. <u>toto</u> m.s.: plug for hole in body-shell.

    k. <u>tsarkiya</u> f.s.: membrane lacing-thongs of gazelle skin secured at their lower end to <u>rik'i</u>, above.

3. In Katsina, the three drums stand vertically on the ground in front of the standing performer, with <u>duma</u> on his left, <u>magu'diya</u> in the middle, and <u>uwar gida</u> on his right; <u>uwar gida</u> and <u>magu'diya</u> are beaten with the right-hand stick or the fingers of the left hand, <u>duma</u> with the fingers of the left hand alone. In Zaria, the two drums stand vertically on the ground in front of the seated performer with the <u>dundufa</u> on his left and the <u>'yar dundufa</u> on his right; they are beaten with a (right) hand-held stick and the fingers of the left hand.

4. Used as a set with three <u>kazagi</u> and one <u>kuntuku</u> or as a set with three <u>kuntuku</u> in the accompaniment of song and/or dancing. In Zaria, used as a set with one or more <u>kuntuku</u>

5. In Katsina, used by men on such occasions as marriage ceremonies, naming ceremonies, and on festivals such as <u>Babbar Salla</u> and <u>K'aramar Salla</u>. In Zaria, used by <u>'yan dundufa</u>, who drum for blacksmiths (<u>mak'era</u>), their traditional patrons.

6. <u>kirarin dundufa</u>:

    <u>Wanda bai san dundufa ba hak'ik'an ya san murya tata</u>
    "He who doesn't actually know <u>dundufa</u> will certainly be familiar with its sound."

<u>ganga</u> m. or f.s. (pl. <u>ganguna</u>)   211.212.1-812
                                           o./no.p.

1. A generic term for any double-membrane cylindrical snared-drum, the most commonly encountered varieties being:

1.1. <u>gangar algaita</u> m. or f.s. ("the <u>ganga</u> for algaita") = <u>k'aramar ganga</u> m. or f.s. ("the small <u>ganga</u>"): after <u>kurya</u> (below), the smallest drum of this genre. Length of body-shell - 13"; diameter of body-shell - 9.5".

1.2. gangar Caji m. or f.s. ("the ganga of Caji"): a
drum of a size intermediate between that of gangar
algaita and gangar fada (below).

1.3. gangar fada m. or f.s. ("the ganga of the palace")
= gangar saraki m. or f.s. ("the ganga of the official"), second in size only to gangar noma (below). Length of body-shell - 17.5"; diameter of
body-shell - 13".

1.4. gangar noma m. or f.s. ("the ganga of farming") =
baragada f.s. = fya'de m.s.: the largest drum of
this genre. Length of body-shell - 26"; diameter
of body-shell - 18".

1.5. kurya f.s.: the smallest drum of this genre.
Length of body-shell - 6.75"; diameter of body-
shell - 8.5".

1.6. kwairama f.s.: about the same size as gangar fada
(above). It frequently has a body-shell made from
a large oil or paint drum.

2. All instruments:

   a. fata f.s. = samfara f.s.: membrane from goat's
   skin.

   b. idan zakara m.s.: small seeds placed inside body-
   shell.

   c. kango m.s. = kwango m.s. = ice m.s.: wooden body-
   shell carved from alulluba or k'irya trees.

   d. kirinya f.s.: hide-ring lapping the membrane.

   e. ma'dauki m.s. = maratayi m.s.: cloth shoulder-
   strap attached to either end of the body-shell.

   f. maka'di m.s. = hurya f.s.: hook-ended drumstick
   from root of gabaruwa tree.

   g. murfi m.s. = mulhi m.s. = rigar ganga f.s.: cloth
   covering the body-shell.

   h. tambari m.s.: rear membrane.

   i. tsarkiya f.s. = tsirkiya f.s.: lacing thongs of
   cow-hide joining the two membranes.

   j. zaga f.s. = zaiga f.s.: snare on front membrane.

k. ceba f.s.: iron jingle attached to upper body-shell of gangar noma only.

3. All instruments are suspended from the left shoulder to lie in a near-horizontal position under the left arm, with the snared membrane to the front (in the case of kurya the membranes are reversed, with the snared membrane to the rear). Either the snared membrane is beaten with the right-hand stick and the fingers of the left hand (this technique being termed hannun gaba), or the snared membrane is beaten with the right-hand stick only, then the rear membrane with the fingers of the left hand (this being termed hannun baya or taushi). Unlike the others, gangar noma is usually beaten with two drumsticks. The gangar noma is also laid on the ground with the rear end tilted up towards the performer's knee, so that the performer bends forward over the drum to strike the front membrane with a drumstick held in each hand, and at the same time, if required, he damps or mutes the rear membrane with his knee (the latter technique being termed taushi).

4. The ensemble combinations and social usages of the various drums of this genre are as follows:

4.1. gangar algaita: used in combination with one or more other gangunan algaita and one or more algaitai (algaita), or with kazagi by the musicians of an Emir, or of his senior officials, in the performance of take in honour of their patron or of his associates. See masu gangar algaita.

4.2. gangar Caji: used in combination with one or more other gangunan Caji, kazagi and kalangu in the accompaniment of popular song by non-official freelance musicians whose performances are in that style known as Caji.

4.3. gangar fada: used by the musicians of an Emir or of his senior officials in the performance of take in honour of their patron or of his associates. In Katsina, such performances under the head of the royal musicians, Sarkin Maka'da, normally involve the synchronic realization of one or more take on a group of gangunan fada, kakakai (kakaki) and farai, in combination with a vocal realization of a kirari by one or more of the drummers. In Zaria, the head of the royal musicians is the Sarkin Busa, and the above ensemble is extended to include one or more k'aho. See sarakuna, marok'an Sarki, marok'an sarakuna.

4.4. gangar noma: used in combination with kazagi by a large class of professional but mainly non-official drummers called masu gangar noma, who beat the take and sing the praises (kirari) of manoma, their principal and traditional patrons. See 'yan hoto, wasan 'yan hoto, gardin kura, wasa da kura, gayya, kalankuwa, rawan Gane, Sarkin Gangar Noma and Sarkin Gangar Noman Zazzau.

4.5. kurya: used by the musicians of an official of an Emir. It is also used by non-official freelance musicians.

4.6. kwairama: used by professional but non-official musicians called masu kwairama, for such entertainments of the youth (samari and 'yan mata) as kokawa, a sha k'afa, rawan Gane, rawan 'yan mata, kai gara and kalankuwa. Drummed solo or in combination with other kwairama and one or more kazagi.

6. As might be expected, there are numerous references to ganga in oral literature, some of the most common being:

   a. Riddle:

   Abu na k'ara a dawa ba hanji -- ganga
   "A thing that cries out in the forest and yet has no guts -- ganga."

   Daga nesa na ji muryar k'awata -- ganga
   "From the distance I hear the voice of my girl-friend -- ganga."

   b. karin magana:

   Idan ka ji ganga na amo (ta cika zak'i) za ta fashe ne
   "When you hear ganga resounding afar (or filled with sweetness) it is about to burst."

   Sai an ci moriyar ganga sa'anan a ke yadda kwango
   "After extracting one's profit from ganga, one discards it in a deserted place."

   Kai bakin ganga ne duk inda aka ta'ba zak'i
   "You are like a double membrane drum, either side beaten will sound sweet," i.e., reference to a two-faced person.

Matsi ka sa ganga zak'i
"Tightening makes the ganga sound sweet," i.e.,
pressure makes difficult persons respond.

c. kirarin kurya:

Kurya, gangar mutuwa
"Kurya, drum of death!"

Kowa sha ki shina barin 'da nai
"Whoever hears you is in the act of leaving his
son (to go to war)."

Ki'di kusa wasa nesa
"When its drumming is near, play is far away."

gangar 'yan kama m. or f.s.   211.241.1
("the gangar of the 'yan kama")   no.p.

1. Single-membrane, snared hourglass drum of fixed
   pitch.

2.a. fata f.s. = fatar tayin dalo f.s.: membrane from
     the foetus of a newly born calf, or from the lungs
     of a cow.

   b. kango m.s. = kwango m.s.: wooden body-shell carv-
      ed from alulluba or k'irya trees.

   c. kungu m.s.: leather ring lapping the membrane,
      made from old membranes.

   d. tsarkiya f.s. = tsirkiya f.s.: leather thongs se-
      curing membrane to a hide-ring around the middle
      of the body-shell.

   e. zaga f.s. = zaiga f.s.: snare from a cow's vein.

3. Suspended from the left shoulder in a near-horizontal position under the left arm so that the membrane
   lies to the front, and beaten with the fingers of
   either hand.

4. Used solo or with other gangunan 'yan kama in the
   accompaniment of recitation and song.

5. Used by 'yan kama in the accompaniment of derisory
   or satirical songs, recitations and actions.

jauje m.s. (pl. jawajawai)   211.242.1-81
                                          o.p.

1. Double membrane hourglass drum of variable pitch
   similar to but larger than kalangu. Length of body-
   shell - 20"; diameter of ends - 9"; diameter of constricted waist - 4".

2.a. dagarya f.s.: hide-ring lapping either membrane.

   b. 'dan kawo m.s.: seed of the kawo tree placed in-
      side the body-shell.

   c. hurya f.s.: hook-ended drumstick from the root of
      the gabaruwa tree.

3. Suspended from the left shoulder in a near-horizontal position between the left upper arm and chest
   with the beaten membrane to the front; the front
   membrane only is beaten, with the right-hand stick
   or the fingers of the left hand, pitch alterations
   being achieved by increasing or decreasing pressure
   on the tensioning thongs running the length of the
   body and joining the two membranes.

4. In combination with up to ten other jawajawai and
   one or more kolaye (kolo) in the performance of take
   and/or the accompaniment of song.

5. Used by the musicians of an Emir, or of his senior
   officials, in the performance of music in honour of
   their patron or his associates. While in Zaria
   jawajawai are owned by the Emir as well as by some
   of his district heads, in Katsina they are owned by
   Galadima, one of the four most senior district heads
   and not by the Emir.

6.a. kirarin jauje:

   Jauje ki'dan mutuwa wanda ba ka taran da'di
   "Jauje, drum of death which you don't encounter
   with pleasure."

kalangu m.s. (pl. kalangai)   211.242.1-81
                                          o.no./p.

1. A generic term for a group of double-membrane hourglass drums of variable pitch similar to but smaller
   than jauje and larger than kolo and 'dan kar'bi, the
   individual instruments being:

1.1. kalangu m.s.: the most commonly found drum of this group, smaller than kalangun Sarki (below) and larger than k'aramar kalangu (below). Length of body-shell - 14"; diameter of ends - 6.5"; diameter of constricted waist - 3".

1.2. kalangun Sarki m.s. ("the kalangu of the Emir"): similar to but larger than kalangu (above).

1.3. k'aramar kalangu m.s. ("the small kalangu"): similar to but smaller than kalangu (above) but larger than the 'dan kar'bi.

2. All instruments:

a. icen kalangu m.s. = kango m.s. = kwango m.s.: wooden body-shell of kalangu, carved from kawo, kimba, k'irya, or marke trees.

b. kambu m.s. = kirinya f.s.: leather-covered lapping ring on membrane.

c. k'angu m.s. = 'dauri m.s.: leather strap attached at one end to the waist of the body-shell and used for tying in the tensioning thongs when the drum is not in use.

d. maka'di m.s.: hook-ended beating stick from the root of the gabaruwa or sanya trees.

e. saisaya f.s.: hide lapping-ring sewn to membrane.

f. samfara f.s.: membrane from young goat's skin.

g. tsarkiya f.s. = tsirkiya f.s.: lacing thongs of cow hide joining the two membranes.

h. tuke m.s.: fine thread of goat's skin used to sew saisaya to samfara.

i. 'ya'yan baba pl. = 'yan'yan kalangu pl.: seeds of baba, kimba, or other plants placed inside body-shell.

3. Suspended from the left shoulder and beaten like jauje. A kalangu drummer also frequently beats 'dan kar'bi at the same time, in which case he may either suspend the latter from his left shoulder so that it lies below kalangu, or more commonly when seated, place 'dan kar'bi across his left knee with the shoulder strap around and under his right knee or around the big toe of his left foot. In both of

these latter cases the pitch of 'dan kar'bi is varied by increasing or decreasing the pull on the
shoulder strap with the right knee or left big toe,
such action being termed tillo.

4. Used solo, in combination with 'dan kar'bi, in combination 'dan kar'bi and kuntuku, also with jita,
kurya, kuge, and kolo. Also in combination with
goge and k'warya; or with kukuma and k'warya. The
k'aramar kalangu is played in combination with
gangar Caji and kazagi of Caji singers and also with
the kazagi and tallabe of 'yan gambara. And in any
or all of these combinations in the accompaniment of
song and/or dancing.

5. The various social usages are as follows:

5.1. kalangu: used most often by a class of professional (usually non-official) musicians called
masu kalangu in various kinds of drumming for
butchers (mahauta), their traditional patrons, and
for the dancing, singing, ceremonies, and games of
the youth. For the latter the drummer beats the
'dan kar'bi together with the kalangu. It is also
used for the accompaniment of freelance singers
such as Alhaji Muhamman Shata. See masu kalangu,
ki'dan mahauta, Sarkin Maka'da.

5.2. kalangun Sarki: In Zaria, and in some other
Emirates, used solo or in combination with kolo or
kuge by an official musician of the Emir (masu
kalangun Sarki) for performance of music in his
honour.

5.3. k'aramar kalangu: used by non-professional freelance musicians performing in market places, sometimes by non-professional musicians drumming for
butchers, and by yaron Caji (yara) and 'yan
gambara.

6.a. karin magana:

Matsi shi ka sa kalangu zak'i
"It's the squeezing makes kalangu sound sweet."

Wane bakin kalangu ne ko ina aka buga sai zak'i
"One is like the mouth of the kalangu, if you beat
either side it will sound loud (sweet)."
(Note: gossipers are called "bakin kalangu" who
"beat" here and "beat" there -- ka buga da nan,
ku buga da nan.)

Ana ruwa ya ci maka'di ku kuna kalangu ya jik'e
"The river drowns the drummer and you are concerned about the kalangu getting wet."

Tun daga somomo inda ka somi duniya kalangu yake
"The kalangu has been in existence since the beginning of the world."

Su wance 'yan baka, kura ta 'dauko kalangu
"Those who are talkative are like a hyena who has
seized a kalangu." (i.e., causing the seeds to
"chatter.")

Kwaram kwatsam mai kalangu ya fa'da a rami
"Suddenly there is a noise of falling objects, the
mai kalangu fell into the hole."

Ba giringirin ba a yi mai kura ta 'dauki kalangu
"Not for the sound but for the meat the hyena
seized the kalangu." (i.e., deeds, not words, are
required.)

kazagi m.s. (pl. kazagai)   211.241.1-812
= kanzagi m.s. (pl. kanzagai)   no.p.

1. Single-membrane snared hourglass drum of fixed
   pitch. Length of body-shell - 9"; diameter of ends
   - 5.5"; diameter of constricted waist - 3.5".

2.a. kango m.s. = kwango m.s.: wooden body-shell carv-
     ed from k'irya tree.

   b. k'angu m.s.: leather strap attached at one end to
      the waist of the body-shell and used for tying-in
      the tensioning thongs to give the drum a fixed
      pitch.

   c. kirinya f.s.: leather covered lapping-ring around
      membrane.

   d. maka'di m.s.: hook-ended drumstick (see also
      'ya'yan kazagi, below).

   e. tsarkiya f.s. = tsirkiya f.s.: lacing thongs of
      gazelle skin, attached at their lower end to turu
      (below).

   f. turu m.s.: leather thong strung through holes
      bored around the edge of the open end of the body-

shell, and used to secure tsarkiya (above) at their lower end.

g. 'ya'yan kazagi pl.: pair of beating thongs made from short lengths of wire wrapped in cloth or leather, or from strips of leather plaited and bound in cloth and finally covered with leather.

h. zaga f.s. = zaiga f.s.: snare across membrane.

3. Either suspended from the player's neck so that it lies in a vertical position at waist level, in which case it is beaten with 'ya'yan kazagi (above), or suspended from the left shoulder so that it lies in a vertical position to one side, in which case it is beaten with one or two maka'di (above).

4. Combined in performance with dundufa, with duma and kurya, with duman girke, with gangar algaita, with gangar noma, with kwairama, or with tallabe, or with any or all of these combinations being in the accompaniment of song and/or dancing.

5. See dundufa, duma, duman girke, gangar algaita, gangar noma, kwairama, 'yan kazagi.

6.a. karin magana:

'Dan kazagi ya fi mai duma 'doki
"The performer on kazagi surpasses the performer on duma in eagerness," (i.e., "It is the lesser member of a partnership who is the keenest.")

b. Riddle:

Ranka bado kan gyeza -- kazagi
"The life of the water lily (the membrane) and the head of the gyeza twig (the snare) -- kazagi."

kolo m.s. (pl. kolaye)   211.242.1.812
                                          o.p.

1. A double-membrane hourglass drum similar to jauje, with which it is normally combined, but smaller and of fixed pitch.

2. See jauje.

3. Held as is jauje, but with the tensioning thongs bound in to give a fixed pitch and normally beaten

only with a stick. A <u>kalangu</u> is also played this
way in combination with the <u>kalangun</u> <u>Sarki</u> and is
similarly called <u>kolo</u>.

4. See <u>jauje</u>.

5. See <u>jauje</u>, <u>masu</u> <u>jauje</u>, <u>marok'an</u> <u>sarakuna</u>, <u>marok'an</u>
   <u>Sarki</u>.

<u>kotso</u> m.s. (pl. <u>kotsanni</u>)   211.241.1-81
                                                          o.p.

1. Single-membrane snared hourglass drum of variable
   pitch. Length of body-shell - 36"; diameter of ends
   - 6"; diameter of constricted waist - 3".

2.a. <u>ice</u> m.s. = <u>kango</u> m.s. = <u>kwango</u> m.s.: wooden body-
     shell carved from <u>alulluba</u> (= <u>alilliba</u>) tree.

   b. <u>kirinya</u> f.s.: leather lapping-ring around mem-
      brane.

   c. <u>k'ofar</u> <u>tsarkiya</u> f.s.: holes drilled around edge
      of open end of body-shell.

   d. <u>mak'ogaro</u> m.s.: open end of body-shell.

   e. <u>ma'dauki</u> m.s. = <u>maratayi</u> m.s.: cloth shoulder
      strap attached to either end of the body-shell.

   f. <u>nake</u> m.s. = <u>nike</u> m.s.: wax layer on membrane
      centre.

   g. <u>samfara</u> f.s. = <u>fatar</u> <u>akwiya</u> f.s.: membrane from
      young goat's skin.

   h. <u>tsarkiya</u> f.s. = <u>tsirkiya</u> f.s.: leather lacing-
      thongs attached at their lower end to <u>k'ofar</u>
      <u>tsarkiya</u> (above).

   i. <u>zaga</u> f.s. = <u>zaiga</u> f.s.: snare on membrane.

3. Suspended from the player's left shoulder so that it
   lies in a near-horizontal position between the left
   upper arm and the chest; beaten with the fingers of
   either hand, on or off the central layer of wax,
   further changes of pitch being effected by increasing or decreasing the pressure of the left upper arm
   on the tensioning thongs running the length of the
   body and securing the membrane at one end to the

holes in the body-shell at the other.

4. Used in combination with one or more other kotsanni in the accompaniment of song.

5. Used by the musicians of an Emir, or of his senior officials for the accompaniment of songs in honour of their patron or his associates. Formerly kotso drummers accompanied the Emir's party into battle and on raiding expeditions. See Masu kotso, marok'an sarakuna, and marok'an Sarki.

6.a. kirarin kotso:

In ka ji kotso kutsa dawa
"Should you hear kotso, melt away into the forest (for an Emir is approaching)."

Kotso mai murya goma
"Kotso, owner of ten voices."

kuntuku m.s. = kurkutu m.s.   211.11-852
= kuttuku m.s. = kuntukuru m.s.   no.p.

1. Single-membrane snared bowl-shaped drum. Length of body-shell - 7"; diameter of open end - 7".

2.a. ice m.s. = kango m.s. = kwango m.s.: wooden body-shell carved from kawo, k'irya or maje trees.

b. ido m.s.: hole in side of body-shell for pouring mixture of oil and spices therein.

c. k'angu m.s.: leather or cloth lapping-ring around membrane made from grass or broom fibres bound in leather or cloth; also leather belt around base of body to which lacing thongs are attached at their lower end, made from plaited thongs or wire bound in leather.

d. tsarkiya f.s. = tsirkiya f.s.: leather lacing-thongs from goat skin.

e. 'yan sanduna pl.: pair of beating sticks, straight or slightly curved.

3. Suspended from the neck so that it lies in a verti-cal position at waist level, or so that it rests in the lap of a seated player, kuntuku is beaten with

the pair of sticks held one in each hand in a rapid
staccato-like style.

4. Used in combination with one or more kalangai
(kalangu) and one 'dan kar'bi in the accompaniment
of song and/or dancing. It is also used in accompaniment of dundufa in Zaria.

5. See kalangu, dundufa, masu kalangu, and 'yan
dundufa.

6.a. karin magana:

Kuntuku ya fi kalangu zak'i
"The kuntuku is louder (sweeter) than the
kalangu."

kuru m.s. (pl. kuwaru)   211.241.1
                                                no.p.

1. Single-membrane snared hourglass drum of fixed
pitch; length of body-shell - 26"; diameter of membrane end - 9"; diameter of open end - 7"; diameter
of constricted waist - 3.5".

3. Held suspended from the left shoulder in a horizontal position at waist level, kuru is beaten with the
fingers of either hand on or off a wax layer at the
centre of the membrane by the drummer who may be
stationary or dancing.

4. Used in combination with up to ten other kuwaru in
the accompaniment of song and/or dancing.

5. As for gangar noma.

tallabe m.s. = gambara f.s.   211.212.1-812
                                                no.p.

1. Double-membrane cylindrical drum. Length of body-
shell - 18"; diameter of ends - 9".

2. As for ganga with exception of the snare.

3. Held suspended from the neck and left shoulder so
that it lies in a horizontal position at waist level
across the front of the body, it is beaten on the
right-hand membrane with a right-hand stick, and on

the other membrane with the fingers of the left
hand.

4. Used in combination with kazagi in the accompaniment
of recitation, song and/or dancing.

5. Used by such performers as 'yan gambara, na uwale,
'yan jarfa (tattooers) and masu wasa da kura.

talle m.s.   211.11
                                              211.311
                                              no.p./np.

Terms used for two sorts of drums:

1.1. Single-membrane drum with a half-gourd body-shell.

1.2. Single-membrane circular frame drum like the
     Yoruba sakara.

3. Held at the edge by the left hand with the fingers
   positioned to mute the membrane, and beaten with a
   right-hand hooked stick.

5. Both used by men in Zaria (maka'dan 'yan tauri) for
   performances in honour of 'yan tauri. They are said
   to have used the kurya as well. Medicine vendors
   often beat talle to advertise their wares.

tambari m.s. (pl. tambura)   211.11-852
                                              o.np.

1. A generic term for a large single-membrane, bowl-
   shaped drum, ownership of which is vested in the office of an Emir or equivalent authority.

1.1. In Zaria two pairs of large tambura called salo-
     salo and 'yan 'dai-'dai and up to two kuntukun
     tambari are played in the 'dakin tambari (house of
     the tambari). The largest member of the set is
     termed giwa. The chiefs of the former vassal
     kingdoms of Kauru, Kajuru, and Lere -- now dis-
     tricts and sub-districts of Zaria Emirate -- also
     have tambura as part of their inherited regalia of
     office. Seven of the tambura of the Emir of Zaria
     and the Chief of Kauru ranged from 17 to 21 inches
     in height and 16 to 21 inches in membrane diame-
     ter. The kuntukun tambari are similarly con-
     structed but smaller: about 11 inches in diameter

and 11 inches in height. None of the tambura or kuntukun tambari of the Emir of Zaria are especially old.

1.2. In the emirate of Abuja, where the pre-Jihad rulers of Zaria are now in residence, the royal regalia includes: two lingarai with bronze body-shells brought to Abuja from Zaria early in the 19th century; and a newer tambari with a wooden body-shell like those of Zaria today. The set are stored and played in the zauren tambari. Lingarai #1 has a membrane diameter of 10-1/2 inches and a height of 8-1/2 inches; Lingarai #2 is 9 inches in diameter and 8-1/2 inches high. The tambari has a membrane diameter of 17-1/2 inches and a height of 18 inches.

In Katsina the following ten royal tambura are owned by the Emir:

1.3. Gwabron Tambari m.s. ("the unique tambari"): the most important tambura captured from the original Court of Katsina during the jihad of Shehu Usuman 'Dan Fodiyo, the drum has a bronze-cased body with a height of 9" and a membrane diameter of 26".

1.33. Lingarai m.s.: like Gwabron Tambari, captured from the original Court of Katsina during the jihad of 'Dan Fodiyo. Height of wooden body - 20"; diameter of membrane - 15".

1.34. Unnamed: likewise captured during the jihad. Height of wooden body - 20"; diameter of membrane - 17".

1.35. Gobir m.s.: captured in the 19th century from the Court of Gobir. Height of wooden body - 19"; diameter of membrane - 16".

1.36. Gamaruga m.s.: presented to the present Emir, Alhaji Sir Usuman Nagogo, on his accession by the Emir of Daura. Height of bronze-cased body - 23"; diameter of membrane - 21".

1.37. Unnamed: like Gamaruga presented by the Emir of Daura.

1.38. Unnamed: presented to Alhaji Muhamman Dikko, father and predecessor of the present Emir, by the Emir of Azben.

1.39. Unnamed: made to commemorate the Queen's visit in 1956.

1.40. Unnamed: likewise made to commemorate the Queen's visit.

1.41. Unnamed: likewise made to commemorate the Queen's visit.

2. All instruments:

  a. akushi m.s. = akwashi m.s.: wooden body-shell carved from ka'danya or maje trees.

  b. daro m.s.: bronze-cased wooden body-shell.

  c. dorina f.s. = bulala f.s.: beating-thongs made from hippopotamus hide.

  d. kayan yaji m.s.: oil and spice mixture poured into body through the hole in the side.

  e. k'irgi m.s.: membrane from bull or cow-hide.

  f. kirinya f.s. = zobe m.s.: iron lacing-ring around base of body-shell.

  g. marfi m.s.: plug for hole in side of body-shell.

  h. rami m.s.: hole in side of body-shell for pouring oil and spice mixture therein.

  i. tada f.s.: tension ligature from cow hide.

  j. tsarkiya f.s. = tsirkiya f.s.: membrane lacing-thongs sewed at their lower end to kirinya, from cow hide.

3. Slightly divergent performance practices obtain in Katsina and Zaria, these being:

3.1. In Katsina, Gwabron Tambari is always beaten on its own with separate strokes from a single dorina, the drum being supported by two men, one on each side, each holding a handle attached to the body-shell. It is beaten only for the installation of the Emir and certain of his officials whose offices are of historical rather than current importance, the number of strokes for each such installation being traditionally prescribed, as is the identity of the official (not musician) performing the beating.

Performances on the other tambura are of two
kinds:

a. Stationary performances in which five tambura
are beaten. Three fork-ended poles are driven
into the ground in a line, two tambura being
hung on each of the two outside poles and one
tambari on the central pole. The central drum
is beaten by Tambura, the official in charge of
these drums, while two of his assistants beat
the two outer pairs of drums, all of the performers using a dorina in either hand. The most
common phrase beaten is:

Kuyangi ko fito da rabanmu ciki
"As for the female slaves -- come out, for our
share is inside!", a phrase deriving from the
tradition that any women found in a public
place while tambura were being beaten immediately became state slaves.

b. Processional performances in which six tambura
are beaten, mounted in pairs on three camels.

3.2. In Zaria, performances on the tambura are of two
kinds:

a. Stationary performances in the 'dakin tambari,
in which two large fork-ended poles are fixed in
the floor, one supporting the 'yan 'dai-'dai and
the other the salo-salo by means of two cowhide
loops attached to each drum. The Sarkin Tambari,
who beats the salo-salo pair, and his assistant,
who beats the 'yan 'dai-'dai, sit on a special
stair-step bench while beating them. The 'yan
'dai-'dai ("one by one") are struck alternately,
maintaining a steady rhythm with either one or
two dorina. The salo-salo ("of different
kinds"), beaten with a dorina in each hand, are
used to express the royal take, the most common
phrase being:

Alhaji 'dan mutanen gabas
"Alhaji, son of the people of Mecca."

One or two kuntukun tambari are placed upright
on the floor and each is beaten by a seated
drummer with a dorina in each hand.

b. For royal cavalcades (hawan salla and hawan
daushe), a pair of tambura are mounted on one

camel and a pair of <u>kuntukun</u> <u>tambura</u> are mounted
on another camel.

4. In Katsina used as a set without the addition of any
other instruments; however, in Zaria, the royal
<u>kakaki</u> is occasionally blown with the <u>tambura</u>.

5. Occasions for beating <u>tambura</u> are traditionally prescribed, and vary considerably between Emirates, as
shown below:

5.1. Daura Emirate

a. When the crescent moon for the month of <u>Rajab</u>
(the 7th Muslim month) is seen. This is the
<u>watan</u> <u>azumin</u> <u>tsoffi</u> or "month of the fast for
old people."

b. At the end of the above month.

c. When the crescent moon for the month of <u>Ramadan</u>
is seen. This is the <u>watan</u> <u>azumin</u> duk <u>gari</u>, or
"month of the fast for all the town."

d. When the above month is over, <u>tambura</u> are beaten
every evening for a week.

e. When the crescent moon for the month of <u>Zul</u> <u>Hajj</u>
(the 12th Muslim month) is seen. This is the
month of the "Great Feast" or <u>Babbar</u> <u>Salla</u>.

f. On the ninth night of <u>Zul</u> <u>Hajj</u>, the eve of
<u>Babbar</u> <u>Salla</u>.

g. On the morning of <u>Babbar</u> <u>Salla</u>.

h. When the crescent moon for the month of <u>Rabi'i</u>
<u>Lawwal</u> (the 3rd Muslim month) is seen. This is
the month of <u>Maulud</u>, the "Prophet's Birthday."

i. On the morning of <u>Maulud</u>.

j. On the eighteenth night of <u>Rabi'i</u> <u>Lawwal</u>, the
eve of <u>Sallar</u> <u>Takutufa</u>, the Prophet's Naming
Day.

k. On the morning of <u>Sallar</u> <u>Takutufa</u>.

l. When the crescent moon for the month of <u>Muharram</u>
(the 1st Muslim month) is seen. This is the
<u>watan</u> <u>wowwo</u>, or the "month of <u>wowwo</u>," the month

in which gifts are exchanged between certain
groups of people (e.g., hunters and scholars,
barbers and blacksmiths, people of Gobir and
Kano, people of Katsina and Zaria, or first
cousins, grandchildren and their grandparents,
etc.) or jokes played on one another by the same
groups of people.

m. On the nineteenth day of Muharram, the day of
wowwo on which the above exchanges take place.

n. On the installation of a new Emir, on which occasion the latter beats the largest tambari himself twelve times.

o. On the installation of either a new Galadima, or
a new K'aura, the two most senior district heads.

5.2. Katsina Emirate

a. On the eve of K'aramar Salla, the feast marking
the end of the month of Ramadan.

b. On the day of K'aramar Salla and thereafter,
morning and evening for a week.

c. On the eve of Babbar Salla, the ninth night of
Zul Hajj.

d. On the day of Babbar Salla and thereafter,
morning and evening for a week.

e. On the installation of a new Emir, on which occasion also the senior District Head, Galadima,
beats Gwabron Tambari twelve times.

f. On the installation of a new K'aura, Galadima,
Durbi, Sarkin Sullu'bawa or 'Yan 'Daka, all senior district heads, Gwabron Tambari alone is
beaten six times in each case by Tambura.

g. On the installation of certain district and village heads, an ordinary tambari alone is beaten
three or four times by Tambura, the number of
strokes depending on the identity of the office.

h. On the conferment of any signal honour on the
Emir a set of tambura are beaten by Tambura and
his assistants.

5.3. Zaria Emirate

a. On the day of K'aramar Salla for the hawan salla
   and thereafter for one month after each of the
   daily prayers and intermittently throughout the
   night, and whenever the Emir leaves the palace
   or returns. The Sarkin Tambari sleeps and eats
   in the 'dakin tambari throughout this month.

b. As above on the day of Babbar Salla and thereafter for one month.

c. For a second royal cavalcade, hawan daushe, held
   two days after each of the feasts of K'aramar
   Salla and Babbar Salla.

d. On the installation of a new Emir and thereafter
   for at least one month.

e. On the installation of a new Madaki, a senior
   official, and thereafter for seven days.

f. On the installation of a new Galadima, a senior
   official, and thereafter for 3 to 7 days.

6. Some idea of the enormous social and political sig-
   nificance of tambura may be obtained from the various traditional and other sayings connected with
   these drums.

   a. kirarin tambari:

   Tambari bugun mutun 'daya
   "Tambari, beaten for one man (the Emir) alone."

   Tambari a ji ka sama
   "Tambari, you are heard (even) in the heavens."

   Tambari wan ganga
   "Tambari, the elder brother of ganga."

   b. Poetry from Gangan Wa'azu:

   Kun san dai matacce ba zai falka ba ko da ana
   ka'da masa gobron tambura
   "You know surely that a dead person will not come
   back to life even if one beats a tambari for
   him."

c. Kirari for victor in foot-boxing contest (a sha k'afa):

Ga mai tambari da sawu ga mai dukan a fa'di
"Here is the tambari drummer, who beats with his foot and knocks his opponent to the ground."

d. Traditional belief:

The tambari is said to beat once by itself when the Emir's successor walks by.

taushi m.s. (pl. tafashe, tausaye)   211.11-852
= tabshi m.s. (pl. tafashe, tabsaye)   o.p.
= zambuna f.s.

1. Single-membrane snared bowl-shaped drum. Length of body-shell - 11"; diameter of membrane - 9".

a. awara f.s.: iron lacing-ring around base of body.

b. danko m.s. = nake m.s.: wax layer on centre of membrane.

c. fata f.s.: membrane from goat or duiker skin.

d. ido m.s.: hole in side of body-shell for pouring oil and spice mixture therein.

e. kirinya f.s.: membrane lapping-ring from rope sewn in leather.

f. ma'dauki m.s.: carrying strap attached to body-shell.

g. taushi m.s.: wooden body-shell carved from faru, kalgo, or k'irya trees.

h. tsarkiya f.s. = tsirkiya f.s.: leather lacing-thongs attached at their lower ends to awara.

i. zaga f.s. = zaiga f.s.: snare on membrane.

3. Either placed in lap of the seated player so that the membrane may be beaten, on or off the wax layer, with the fingers of either hand, or carried suspended from the left shoulder so that the membrane may be similarly beaten.

4. Used with one or more other tafashe in the accompaniment of song.

5. Used by the musicians of an Emir or senior official for the accompaniment of songs in honour of their patron or his associates. See masu taushi, marok'an sarakuna, marok'an Sarki.

turu m.s. (pl. turaye)	211.211.1-8 or 211.212.1-812 no.np.

1. Small single- or double-membrane cylindrical drum with a body-shell made from a tin-can or other suitable container.

3. Beaten with the fingers of either hand.

4. Used on its own or in the accompaniment of informal song.

5. Used by children for self-amusement.

zambuna f.s. and pl.	211.261.2-8 o.p.

1. Pair of unique, single-membrane, goblet-shaped drums with closed ends.

3. Suspended from the left shoulder so that each lies in a near horizontal position at waist level with the membrane to the front. Beaten with a right-hand stick and the fingers of the left hand.

4. Used as a set for the performance of take and/or the accompaniment of song.

5. Ownership of zambuna is vested in the office of Mara'di, the Village Head of Kurfi in Katsina Emirate, for whom they are traditionally beaten.

6.a. kirarin zambuna:

Da ka mutu mi ka bari -- sa'ba'ba
"When you die, what do you leave -- a hopeless mess."

Mak'i maganar banza na Abu
"Hater of worthless chatter, one of Abu."

3) Chordophones

garaya f.s. (pl. garayu)   321.311-6
                                            no.p.

1. Generic term for a two-stringed plucked lute occurring in two main sizes, as below:

1.1. garaya f.s.:   the smallest member of this family,
     with a carved ovoid wooden body-resonator. Over-
     all length, including neck - 22"; length of ex-
     posed neck - 12"; length of vibrating strings -
     16".

1.2. babbar garaya f.s. (the "big garaya") = komo m.s.:
     the largest member of this family, with an ovoid
     gourd body-resonator. Overall length, including
     neck and iron jingle at the end thereof - 70";
     length of jingle - 30"; length of exposed neck -
     22"; length of vibrating strings - 32".

2.a. amale m.s. ("huge camel") = giwa f.s. ("elephant")
     = tambari m.s.:   the lowest pitched of the two
     strings, each with the same vibrating length but
     tuned at an interval of approximately 500 cents.

   b. ceba f.s.:   long, rectangular iron jingle with
      small wire rings set into holes around its edge;
      attached to the end of the neck of babbar garaya.

   c. farke m.s. = farko m.s.:   small leather plectrum
      from cow's hide.

   d. fata f.s.:   membrane covering body-resonator from
      goat or duiker skin.

   e. kallabi m.s.:   leather thongs binding strings to
      neck.

   f. k'ok'on garaya m.s.:   body-resonator of the small
      garaya.

   g. komo m.s.:   body-resonator of babbar garaya or
      komo.

   h. kurman laya m.s.:   talisman attached to neck of
      garaya, usually a written passage from the Koran
      sewn in a leather pouch.

i. magu'diya f.s. (the "ululator"): the highest-
   pitched of the two vibrating strings.

j. sandar gamu m.s.: the neck.

k. tsarkiya f.s. = tsirkiya f.s.: generic for both
   vibrating strings on either instrument.

3. The instrument is held at the neck-end by the left
   hand with the fingers in position to stop either
   string; the body-resonator rests against the player's waist, or in his lap if seated, and the strings
   are plucked with the right-hand plectrum.

4. Used solo with caki, or kasam'bara, or with caki or
   kasam'bara in the joint accompaniment of song and/or
   dancing; solo with one or more other garayu and caki
   or kasam'bara, or as a group in the accompaniment of
   song and/or dancing.

5. Used by men for the performance of music of various
   types. Originally garaya was used for music in honour of hunters, and in particular for praising hunters in their traditional rivalry with malamai; it is
   today less restricted in use and is employed for
   such different types of music as songs of entertainment (wak'ar nasha'di), praise songs (wak'ar yabo)
   and songs of possession (wak'ar bori). In Zaria the
   garaya is used mainly for bori ceremonies, and the
   komo or babbar garaya is played for hunters
   (maharba). See masu garaya and masu komo.

6.a. kirarin garaya:

   Gangar maharba
   "Drum of the hunters"

   Garaya kim fi mugunyar mata
   "Garaya, you are better than a bad woman."

goge m.s. (pl. goguna)   321.311-71
                                               no.p.

1. Single-stringed bowed lute. Overall length - 26";
   length of exposed neck - 15"; length of vibrating
   string - 15".

2.a. fata f.s.: membrane covering body-resonator from
   the skin of the Nile monitor.

b. izga f.s. = yazga f.s. = tambara f.s.: iron- or bronze-backed bow with hairs from a horse's tail.

c. jaki m.s.: bridge between string and body-resonator from a three-pronged twig of the urkure tree.

d. k'ahon butsiya m.s.: small horn-like wedge inserted between lower end of string and body-resonator to increase tension of former.

e. kallabi m.s.: leather binding thongs securing strings at upper end to neck.

f. k'ank'ara f.s.: smooth egg-shaped stone inserted under membrane-covering of body-resonator to increase tension of the former.

g. kanwa f.s.: potash used to remove the natural oils from the body and bow-strings.

h. k'aro m.s.: resin for body and bow strings from Copaiba balsam tree.

i. kumbo m.s.: hemispherical body-resonator from a latitudinally cut half-gourd.

j. tsagiya f.s.: string on body-resonator from hairs from a horse's tail.

k. wuri m.s.: a cowrie-shell used like k'ank'ara, above.

3. Held at the neck-end by the left hand with the fingers in position to stop the string; the body-resonator rests against the player's waist, or in his lap if seated, and the string is bowed with a nearly vertical up and down action by the right hand bow.

4. Used solo, solo with one or more k'warya, solo with one or more kalangu and 'dan kar'bi, or with combinations of the above in the joint accompaniment of songs and/or dancing.

5. Used by men for the performance of music of various types, e.g., songs of entertainment (wak'ar nasha'di), songs of praise (wak'ar yabo), political songs (wak'ar siyasa), possession songs (wak'ar bori). Made immensely popular by the artistry of such performers as Audu Yaron Goge and Garba Liyo. See masu goge, bori, rawan kashewa, Sarkin Goge.

6.a. kirarin goge:

Yazgar marigyayi ko malan ba ya cewa ba da'di sai
dai ya ce babu kyau
"Hairs of the dead horse, not even a religious
teacher can say you are not sweet to the ear, he
can only say you are not edifying."

Goge mai kashe wa molo kaifi
"Goge who silences the mob" (i.e., it is louder).

Goge ki'dan 'yan duniya ne
"Goge is the music of worldly people."

Goge kan bidi'a ke nan
"Goge is the source of heresy."

gurmi m.s. = kumbo m.s.   321.311-5
                                            no.p.

1. Two-stringed plucked lute with hemispherical body-
   resonator. Overall length, including neck - 24";
   length of exposed neck - 18"; diameter of body-resonator - 6"; length of vibrating strings - 18".

2.a. amale m.s. (the "huge camel") = giwa f.s. (the
     "elephant") = tambari m.s.: the lowest pitched of
     the two strings, each made from twisted hairs from
     a horse's tail and tuned at an interval approach-
     ing 700 cents.

   b. fata f.s.: membrane covering body-resonator, from
      skin of land monitor.

   c. kallabi m.s.: leather binding-thongs securing
      strings at their upper end to the neck.

   d. kara f.s.: bridge between vibrating strings and
      membrane-covering of body-resonator, from a short
      length of guinea corn stalk with 'ya'yan baba in-
      serted in ends.

   e. kumbo m.s. = kurtu m.s.: hemispherical body-reso-
      nator from a latitudinally cut half-gourd.

   f. magu'diya f.s. (the "ululator"): highest pitched
      of the two vibrating strings.

   g. tsarkiya f.s. = tsirkiya f.s.: generic for both
      vibrating strings.

h. 'ya'yan baba pl.: seeds of the indigo plant inserted in either end of the bridge to give a char-
acteristic "buzzing" sound to the instrument.

3. Held as for garaya, with the lowest-pitched string
uppermost; the lowest-pitched string is plucked with
the right-hand thumb, and the highest-pitched string
with the right-hand index finger.

4. Used solo or in the accompaniment of song.

5. Used by men for various types of music, but especially sung in praise of 'yan kokuwa. See masu
gurmi.

jita m.s. (d.f. English, guitar)   321.322-6
           no.p.

1. Imported western guitar.

3. Normal technique.

4. Used as an accompaniment instrument in solo singing.

kukuma f.s. (pl. kukumai)   321.311-71
           no.p.

1. Single-stringed bowed lute similar to, but smaller
than goge. Overall length including neck - 20";
length of exposed neck - 12"; length of vibrating
string - 9.5".

2. As for goge, with the exception of:

a. jaki m.s.: bridge inserted between string and
membrane covering body-resonator, from a "u"
shaped section of guinea corn stalk cut from the
top of the plant as it bends over before harvesting.

b. k'ahon mariri m.s.: small oryx horn used as a
wedge between the string at its lower end and the
body-resonator in order to increase the tension of
the former.

3. As for goge, except that the body-resonator rests
closer to the chest than the waist.

4. As for _goge_.

5. Made popular by the artistry of such performers as Ibrahim Na Habu and Ali 'Dan Saraki. Used as is _goge_ but by men and women and professionals and non-professionals. See _masu kukuma_, _masu wak'ar kukuma_.

6.a. _karin magana_:

   Abin da ya kai tsafuwa rawar kukuma -- tare jelanta
   "What made the old woman dance to _kukuma_ was that she was collecting her tail feathers," i.e., "No one acts without a motive, however ridiculous."

---

kuntigi m.s. (pl. _kuntuga_)   321.311-6
= _kuntugi_ m.s.   no.p./np.

1. Single-stringed plucked lute. Overall length, including neck - 12.5"; length of exposed neck - 6.5"; length of vibrating string - 11".

2.a. _ceba_ f.s.: metal jingle attached to end of neck on some instruments but not used by such well-known performers as 'Dan Maraya and Mai Kur'di 'Dan Duna.

   b. _gora_ f.s.: neck from a length of thin bamboo.

   c. _gwangwanin kifi_ m.s.: body-resonator from an o-void herring tin with the top removed, or from a sardine tin.

   d. _tantanin dalo_ m.s.: membrane covering body-resonator from calf's skin.

   e. _tsagiya_ f.s.: string from twisted camel hairs.

3. Held as for _garaya_, but with the body-resonator closer to the chest than to the waist; plucked with a right-hand plectrum from the quill of a vulture's feather.

4. Solo in the accompaniment of song, or with one or more other _kuntuga_ in the accompaniment of song.

5. Used by men and, less often, by women for the accompaniment of various types of song, e.g., songs of entertainment (wak'ar nasha'di), political songs (wak'ar siyasa) and praise songs (wak'ar yabo). See masu kuntigi.

molo m.s. (pl. molaye)   321.311-5
= tafashe m.s.   no.p./np.

1. Three-stringed plucked lute. Overall length, including neck - 27"; length of exposed neck - 10"; lengths of vibrating strings - 14", 22", 22".

2.a. amale m.s. (the "huge camel") = giwa f.s. (the "elephant") = tambari m.s.: the lowest pitched of the three strings tuned at intervals approaching 500 and 700 cents upwards (i.e., so that the highest string is approximately an octave above the lowest), and each made from hairs from a horse's tail twisted together.

   b. fata f.s.: membrane covering body-resonator from goat's or duiker skin.

   c. gora f.s.: neck from a length of thin bamboo.

   d. ice m.s.: wooden body-resonator carved to a trough-like shape from the tumfafiya tree.

   e. kallabi m.s.: leather thongs securing the strings to the neck.

   f. magu'diya f.s. (the "ululator"): shortest and highest pitched of the three strings.

   g. sha ki'di m.s. ("undergo the beating"): the middle-pitched of the three strings.

   h. tsarkiya f.s. = tsirkiya f.s.: generic for any of the three strings.

3. Held as for garaya, except that the shortest string is not stopped but supplies a drone; the lowest pitched string is plucked with the thumb of the right hand, and sha ki'di with the index finger, all fingers of the right hand being used to tap the membrane covering the resonator periodically.

4. Used solo, solo with caki or kasam'bara, or in combinations of the above in the joint accompaniment of
song.

5. Used by men, both amateurs and professionals, for
the accompaniment of various kinds of song, but traditionally for the accompaniment of songs in praise
of famous warriors. See masu molo.

4) Aerophones

algaita f.s. (d.f. Arabic al raita);   422.112-7
(pl. algaitai) = raha f.s.   o.p.

1. Double-reed vibrated pipe of conical bore. Length,
including mouthpiece and reeds - 21"; diameter of
mouthpiece bore - .5"; diameter of lower end of
pipe - 2.5".

2.a. algaita f.s.: wooden bell-ended pipe carved from
daniya tree.

b. garkuwa f.s.: round brass disc forming end of
reed-holder.

c. haki m.s. = macara f.s. = sheme m.s.: double-reed
cut from suitable grass stalk and prepared by
boiling with meat fat, onions and spices.

d. jakar algaita f.s.: leather carrying-bag.

e. kwarkwaro m.s.: complete brass reed-holder including garkuwa, above.

f. tsahi m.s.: narrow-bore of neck of pipe.

g. wutaci m.s.: each of the four fingerholes bored
in the wooden pipe.

3. Held by both hands in a near-horizontal position,
with the left hand positioned towards the bell end.
The fingerholes are stopped by the index finger of
the right hand and the index, second and third fingers of the left hand, and the instrument is blown
with the cheeks acting as an air reservoir.

4. Used solo with gangar algaita or with one or more other algaitai and gangunan algaita or with kakakai (kakaki), farai and gangar fada.

5. Used by musicians of senior officials, not of the Emir in Katsina and Zaria, for the performance of take and in the accompaniment of songs of praise in honour of their patron or their associates. See masu algaita, marok'an sarakuna, Magajin Busa and Sarkin Maka'da.

begila f.s. (d.f. English, bugle)   423.121.12
                                                 no.np.

1. Imported Western military bugle.

3. Normal technique.

4. Normal band combinations.

5. Normal band usage.

bututu m.s.   423.121.11

1. Lip-vibrated end-blown pipe formed from a length of a hollow stem of a pawpaw leaf.

5. Used by children for self-amusement.

damalgo m.s.   422.31
                                                 no.np.

1. A transversely blown, single beating-reed, idioglot pipe which is similar to til'boro but larger, with a finger hole and a gourd resonance chamber on the distal end of the tube.

2. As for the til'boro, except for the following:

   a. damalgo: two sections of guinea corn stalk cut to form a pipe open at both ends, 21" in length.

   b. k'ok'o = k'ok'uwa: small round calabash resonance chamber about 3" in diameter with a hole cut in its side to attach it to the distal end of the pipe. There are four other holes cut into its surface, each about 1/2" in diameter, permitting the escape of sound.

3. As with til'boro, except the finger hole at the distal end of the pipe is stopped with the left thumb.

4. Solo or in the accompaniment of song and dance.

5. Used by young men for their own pleasure or to earn small change, especially during the month of Ramadan. See 'yan damalgo.

farai m.s. = famfami m.s.   423.121.12
(pl. famfamai)   o.p.

1. Wooden, lip-vibrated, end-blown pipe. Length - 32"; bore at mouthpiece - .5"; bore at bell end - 2.5".

2.a. falami m.s. = fallami m.s.: wooden mouthpiece section carved from alilliba or gwandar jeji trees.

   b. gora f.s.: middle section from a length of bamboo.

   c. k'ofa f.s.: bore of mouthpiece.

   d. maratayi m.s.: cloth carrying-strap.

   e. rami m.s.: bore of middle and end-sections.

   f. turmi m.s.: bell-end section, carved from wood of alilliba tree or formed from metal from a kerosine tin.

3. Held to the mouth in a near-horizontal position by the player's right hand at the mouthpiece end and left hand near the bell end.

4. In combination with kakakai (kakaki), gangar fada, and, in Zaria, k'aho.

5. Used by the musicians of an Emir for the performance of praises in honour of their patron, though musicians of other senior officials in Zaria formerly used them. See masu farai and Magajin Busa.

6.a. kirarin farai:

Farai busan mutun 'daya
"Farai, blown for one man alone (the Emir)."

k'aho m.s. (pl. k'ahoni)   423.122.2
                                    o.p.

1. Side-blown lip-vibrated animal horn.

2.a. k'ofa f.s.: embouchure, cut into side of horn
close to lip.

  b. maratayi m.s.: cord carrying-strap.

  c. shata f.s.: horn of the female roan antelope used
to construct the instrument body.

  d. turmi m.s.: bell-end from oxhorn attached to
shata with beeswax.

3. Held to the mouth in a near-horizontal position with
the right hand near the tip and the left hand towards the bell end. The forefinger stops the open
tip end and the fingers of the left hand are placed
over the bell end.

4. Solo or in combination with kakaki, farai and gangar
fada.

5. Used by the musicians of an Emir for the performance
of praises in honour of their patron. In Zaria it
was also formerly used by other senior officials.
See masu k'aho, Sarkin Busa, marok'an sarakuna,
marok'an Sarki.

kakaki m.s. (d.f. Songhay ?)   423.121.12
(pl. kakakai)   o.p.

1. Long, metal, lip-vibrated, end-blown pipe in two de-
tachable sections. Overall length between 8 feet
and 14 feet, depending on the area, the following
measurements applying to an average instrument in
Katsina: overall length - 97"; length of mouthpiece
section - 48"; length of bell-end section - 49";
bore at mouthpiece - 1"; bore immediately before ac-

tual bell end - 2.75"; maximum diameter of bell end
- 4".

2.a. home m.s.: actual bell end from metal of kerosine
  tin or thin brass.

 b. jakar kakaki f.s.: leather or cloth carrying-bag.

 c. karan kakaki m.s.: the long thin part of the
  mouthpiece section from metal of kerosine tin or
  thin brass.

 d. magu'diya f.s. (the "ululator"): actual mouthpiece from metal of kerosine tin or thin brass.

 e. uwa f.s. (the "mother"): complete bell-end section from metal of kerosine tin or thin brass.

 f. 'ya f.s. (the "daughter"): complete mouthpiece
  section.

3. Held to the mouth in a near-horizontal position with
   the right hand near the mouthpiece and the extended
   left arm towards the bell end. Blown to produce two
   notes approximately 750 cents apart; a third note at
   an interval of approximately 100 cents below the
   lowest of the two previous notes, is less commonly
   used. When a group of kakakai are used for "solo
   and chorus" type performance, the "chorus" instruments are approximately 100 cents higher in pitch
   than the "solo" instrument throughout their range.

4. Used solo, solo with one or more other kakakai, as a
   group with gangar fada, as a group with gangar fada
   and farai, and as a group with gangar fada, farai
   and k'aho. Occasionally the Sarkin Kakaki of the
   Emir of Zaria plays with tambura. All the above
   performances being based on the instrumental realization of one or more take and the vocal realization
   of a kirari.

5. Used by the musicians of an Emir for performances in
   honour of their patron or his associates. More
   rarely, as in Zaria, kakaki may be owned by a lesser
   official but, if so, only with the approval of the
   Emir. See masu kakaki, Sarkin Busa, marok'an
   sarakuna.

6.a. kirarin kakaki:

   Kakaki busan mutun 'daya
   "Kakaki, blown for one man alone (the Emir)."

Barawon <u>kakaki</u> <u>ba</u> <u>shi</u> <u>da</u> <u>iko</u> <u>ya</u> <u>busa</u> <u>shi</u>
"The man who steals <u>kakaki</u> still does not have the
authority to blow it."

<u>sarewa</u> f.s. = <u>mabusa</u> f.s.   421.111.12
= <u>sheshe</u> m.s.   no.p./np.

1. End-blown flute with four finger-holes. Overall
   length - 22"; bore - 1". Cut from length of guinea
   corn stalk and bound with the bark of the <u>kalgo</u>
   tree.

3. Held in a near-vertical position with the left hand
   above the right hand, the index and third fingers of
   both hands being used for stopping, the instrument
   is blown out of the side of the mouth.

4. Used solo, solo with <u>kasam'bara</u>, or with <u>kasam'bara</u>
   in the joint accompaniment of song.

5. Used by men for cattle herding or, less commonly,
   for music for entertainment (<u>wak'ar</u> <u>nasha'di</u>) or
   possession (<u>wak'ar</u> <u>bori</u>). See <u>masu</u> <u>sarewa</u>.

<u>til'boro</u> m.s. = <u>tillik'o</u> m.s.   422.31
= <u>tillik'oro</u> m.s. = <u>obati</u> m.s.   no.np.

1. A transversely blown, single beating-reed, idioglot
   pipe.

2.a. <u>belu</u> m.s. = <u>beli</u> m.s.: reed cut from section of
     actual pipe near closed end of latter.

   b. <u>til'boro</u> m.s.: section of guinea-corn stalk cut
      to form a pipe open at both ends, about 1 foot in
      length and 1/2" in diameter.

   c. <u>zare</u> m.s.: a piece of thread tied loosely around
      the vibrating reed to control the movement of the
      latter.

3. Held to the mouth so that it covers the reed, the
   pipe being in a near-horizontal position with the
   right hand at the reed end and the left hand at
   the open end. The reed is vibrated by either
   blowing or sucking, the index finger of the

left hand being used to stop the open end of the pipe.

4. Used solo or with other til'boro.

5. Used by children and young men for amusement.

B. TERMS FOR PARTS OF INSTRUMENTS

While terms referring to parts of instruments are listed under the instruments to which they belong, they do as a body demonstrate a certain standardization of terminology not only among instruments of the same genre, but also among those from completely different families. For this reason all such terms, whether standardized or not, have been extracted and are presented in a list immediately hereunder, together with a brief description of their general provenance:

akushi m.s. ("a large wooden bowl") = akwashi m.s.: wooden body-shell of tambari carved from ka'danya or maje trees.

algaita f.s.: wooden body of the aerophone of that name carved from daniya tree.

amale m.s. ("a large camel"): lowest pitched of the strings on garaya, gurmi, and molo and also termed giwa and tambari.

awara f.s.: iron lacing-ring around the base of banga and taushi.

banga f.s.: wooden body-shell of the drum of that name, carved from alilliba (= aluluba), katsari or k'irya trees.

belu m.s. = beli m.s.: beating reed cut from section of guinea corn stalk or til'boro.

bulala f.s.: hippopotamus-hide beating thongs used on tambari and more specifically termed dorina.

buta f.s.: bottle-shaped gourd used for body of the rattle known as caki.

ceba f.s.: jingle from a length of thin metal pierced a-
round its edges with wire rings, attached to
kwairama, gangar noma, garaya, and some examples of
kuntigi.

cinki m.s. = tsinke m.s.: large iron needle for replacing
membranes, and attached to the side of that member
of the dundufa drum set known as magu'diya.

dagarya f.s.: hide-lapping ring around membrane on jauje.

'dan kawo m.s.: seeds of the kawo tree placed inside the
body-shell of jauje.

danko m.s.: wax layer on centre of membrane of taushi;
also termed nake.

daro m.s. ("a metal basin") = bronze-cased wooden body-
shell of certain examples of tambari.

dauri m.s.: leather strap attached at one end to the constricted waist of kalangu and 'dan kar'bi drums and
used for tying in the tensioning thongs when the
drums are not in use or when a fixed pitch is required; also termed k'angu.

dorina f.s.: specific term for hippopotamus-hide beating
thongs used on tambari and also known as bulala.

duma m.s.: generic for a number of kinds of gourd among
which are the bottle-shaped gourd used as a body for
the rattle caki, and the large barrel-shaped gourds
used for the body-shells of the drums forming the
duma and duman girke sets.

falami m.s. = fallami m.s.: wooden mouthpiece section of
farai carved from alliliba (= aluluba) or gwandar
jeji trees.

farke m.s. = farko m.s.: small leather plectrum from
cow's hide used with garaya.

fata f.s.: generic term for the membrane on such drums as
banga, duma, duman girke, dundufa, ganga, gangar
'yan kama, kotso, and taushi; also generic for the
membrane covering on the body-resonators of such
stringed instruments as garaya, goge, gurmi, and
molo.

furya f.s.: wooden body-shells of the drums belonging to
the set known as dundufa carved from alliliba
(= aluluba), kawo or k'irya trees.

galura f.s. = garura f.s.: bottle-shaped gourd used for
the body of the rattle known as caki.

garkuwa f.s.: round brass disc forming end of reed-holder
on algaita.

giwa f.s.: lowest-pitched of the strings on garaya, gurmi
and molo; also termed amale and tambari.

gora f.s.: length of bamboo used as a neck for kuntigi
and molo and for the middle section of farai.

gwangwanin kifi m.s.: ovoid herring or sardine tin used
as a body-resonator for kuntigi.

gyan'dama f.s.: bottle-shaped gourd used as a body for
the rattle known as caki.

haki m.s.: double-reed cut from a length of grass stalk,
boiled with meat fat, onions and spices, and used
for algaita; also termed macara and sheme.

home m.s.: bell-end of kakaki made from kerosine tin or
thin brass pan.

hurya f.s.: beating-stick for such drums as dundufa,
ganga, and jauje, from aduwa, geza or sabara trees
or if hook-ended from root of gabaruwa tree; also
termed maka'di.

ice m.s.: wooden body-shell of such drums as ganga,
kalangu, kotso and kuntuku and wooden body-resonator
of molo; carved from such trees as alliliba
(= aluluba), kawo, kimba, k'irya, maje, marke, and
in the case of molo, tumfafiya tree; in the case of
drums also termed kango (= kwango).

idon zakara m.s.: small seeds placed inside body-shell of
ganga.

ido m.s.: hole in the side of the body-shell of such
drums as dundufa, kuntuku, and taushi; also termed
k'ofa.

izga f.s. = yazga f.s.: iron- or bronze-backed bow with
string from the hairs of a horse's tail, used on
goge and kukuma; also termed tambara.

jaka f.s.: leather carrying-bag for algaita and kakaki.

jaki m.s.: bridge between membrane on body-resonator and
string on goge and kukuma, in the former case from a
three-pronged twig of the urkuru tree, in the latter
case from the "u" shaped stalk cut from the top of a
guinea-corn plant as it bends before harvesting.

kafar zuba mai f.s.: hole in the side of the body-shell
of banga; also termed k'ofar zuba mai.

k'aho m.s.: small horn used as a wedge for increasing the
tension of the string on goge and kukuma.

kallabi m.s.: leather thong binding the string or strings
to the neck on such instruments as garaya, goge,
gurmi, and molo.

kambu m.s.: leather lapping-ring around the membrane of
kalangu; also termed kirinya.

kango m.s. = kwango m.s.: wooden body-shell of such drums
as dundufa, ganga, gangar 'yan kama, kalangu,
kazagi, kotso, and kuntuku; carved from alliliba,
kawo, k'irya, kimba, marke, and maje trees; also
termed ice.

k'angu m.s.: leather-strap attached to the constricted
waist of such drums as kalangu, 'dan kar'bi and
kazagi, and used to tie the tensioning cords in when
not in use, or when a constant pitch is required;
also termed 'dauri.

k'ank'ara f.s.: smooth egg-shaped stone inverted under
membrane covering of body-resonator to increase the
tension of the former, on such instruments as goge
and kukuma.

kan tandu m.s.: base of the instrument known as tandu.

kanwa f.s.: potash used to remove the natural oils from
the body and bow-strings of goge and kukuma.

kara f.s.: bridge from a short length of guinea-corn
stalk with seeds of the indigo plant inserted in the
ends, used on gurmi; the long thin tube of the
mouthpiece section of kakaki, made from kerosine
tins or thin brass pans.

k'aro m.s.: resin for body and bow-strings of goge and
kukuma, from the Copaiba balsam tree.

kayan yaji m.s.: oil and spice mixture poured through a
hole in the side of tambari; made from man shanu
("butter"), zuma ("honey") and barkono ("red pep-
per"), citta mai kwaya, fasakwari, citta kulla,
karamfani, citta mai yatsu, kimba, masoro, as well
as albasa ("onions").

kirgi m.s.: membrane from bull- or cow-hide on tambari.

kirinya f.s.: hide-ring lapping the membrane on such
drums as banga, dundufa, ganga, kalangu, kazagi,
kotso, and taushi; also iron lacing-ring around base
of tambari, also termed zobe.

k'ofa f.s.: bore of embouchure of such instruments as
farai and k'aho.

k'ofar tsarkiya f.s.: holes drilled around edge of open
end of body-shell of kotso for securing lacing-
thongs.

k'ofar zuba mai f.s.: hole drilled in side of body-shell
of such drums as banga and dundufa.

k'ok'o m.s.: cut gourd used as body-resonator of the
small garaya.

komo m.s.: cut gourd used as body-resonator of the large
garaya or komo.

kumbo m.s.: cut gourd used as body-resonator of goge and
and gurmi; also termed kurtu.

k'ungu m.s.: leather lapping-ring around membrane of such
drums as gangar 'yan kama and kuntuku.

kurman laya m.s.: talisman attached to the neck of garaya
and made from a written passage from the Koran sewn
up in a leather pouch.

kurtu m.s.: cut gourd used as body-resonator of gurmi;
also termed kumbo.

kwarkwaro m.s.: complete brass reed-holder of algaita.

liko m.s.: plug for the hole in the side of the body-
shell of banga.

ma'dauki m.s.: carrying-strap on such drums as banga,
ganga, kotso and taushi; also termed maratayi.

magu'diya f.s.: highest pitched of the strings on garaya,
     gurmi, and molo, and the mouthpiece of kakaki.

maka'di m.s.: beating stick for such drums as dundufa,
     ganga, kalangu, and kazagi; if straight, from aduwa,
     geza or sabara trees; if hook-ended, from root of
     gabaruwa or sanya trees; also termed hurya or gula.

mak'ogaro m.s.: open end of body-shell of kotso.

man gya'da m.s.: ground-nut oil poured through hole in
     side of body-shell of dundufa.

maratayi m.s.: carrying-strap on such drums as banga,
     ganga, kotso, and on such aerophones as farai and
     k'aho.

marfi m.s.: plug for the hole in the side of tambari.

murfi m.s. = mulhi m.s.: cloth covering body-shell of
     ganga.

nake m.s. = nike m.s.: wax layer on centre of membrane of
     such drums as banga, kotso and taushi; made from
     finely sifted laterite subsoil and pounded fruit of
     the aduwa (date palm) tree; also termed dank'o.

rami m.s.: hole in side of body-shell of tambari and bore
     of middle and end sections of farai.

rici m.s.: membrane lacing-thongs on banga.

riga f.s.: cloth covering body-shell of such drums as
     banga and gangar fada; also termed murfi.

rik'i m.s.: leather or iron lacing-ring around the base
     of such drums as dundufa.

saisaya f.s.: hide lapping-ring sewn to membrane of
     kalangu and 'dan kar'bi.

samfara f.s.: thin membrane on such drums as ganga,
     kalangu and kotso; from the skin of a young goat;
     also termed fata.

sandar gamu m.s.: the neck of garaya.

sha ki'di m.s.: the middle-pitched of the three strings
     on molo.

shata f.s.: horn of the female roan antelope, used for
     the body of k'aho.

ta'barya f.s.: pestle used with turmi

ta'da f.s.: tension ligature on tambari.

tambara f.s.: iron- or bronze-backed bow with string from
hairs from a horse's tail, used on goge and kukuma.

tantanin dalo m.s.: membrane covering body-resonator of
kuntigi, from calf-skin.

taushi m.s.: wooden body-shell of the drum of that name,
carved from faru, kalgo, or k'irya trees.

til'boro m.s.: body of the pipe known by that name.

toto m.s.: plug for the hole in the side of the body-
shell of dundufa.

tsagiya f.s.: string of goge, kukuma and kuntigi, in the
two former cases from the hairs from a horse's tail,
in the last from camel hairs.

tsahi f.s.: narrow bore of the neck of the pipe known as
algaita.

tsarkiya f.s.: membrane lacing-thongs on such drums as
dundufa, ganga, gangar 'yan kama, kalangu, kazagi,
kotso, kuntuku, tambari, taushi and generic for the
strings on such instruments as garaya and molo.

tuke m.s.: fine thread of goat's skin used to sew saisaya
to samfara on kalangu.

turmi m.s.: bell-end section of farai and k'aho.

turu m.s.: leather thong strung through the holes around
the open end of kazagi and used for securing lacing-
thongs.

uwa f.s.: complete bell-end section of kakaki, from kerosine tin or thin brass pan.

wuri m.s.: a cowrie shell inserted under membrane covering on goge and kukuma to increase the tension of
the covering.

'yan sanduna pl.: pair of beating-sticks used on kuntuku.

'ya'yan baba pl.: seeds of indigo plant placed inside
body-shell of kalangu and in ends of bridge on
gurmi.

zaga f.s. = zaiga f.s.: snare on membrane of such drums
     as ganga, gangar 'yan kama, kazagi, kotso and
     taushi.

zare m.s.: piece of thread tied loosely around the vi-
     brating reed of til'boro.

zobe m.s.: iron lacing-ring around base of body-shell of
     tambari, also termed kirinya.

II. Professional Performers

A. COLLECTIVE TERMS

B. CLASSES OF PERFORMERS

1) Masu ki'da ("drummers")
   a. Idiophonists ("Drummers on idiophones")
   b. Drummers
   c. Lutenists ("Drummers on chordophones")

2) Masu busa ("blowers")

3) Mawak'a ("singers")

4) Marok'an baki ("acclamators")

5) 'Yan magana ("talkers")

C. OFFICES AND TITLES OF PERFORMERS

A. COLLECTIVE TERMS

mabusa, masu busa pl. (mai busa m.s.)
= mabusa pl. (mabushi m.s.)

Performers on aerophones.

magu'da pl. (magu'diya f.s.)

Women specializing in celebratory ululating.

See gu'da.

maka'da pl. (maka'di m.s.)
= masu ki'da pl. (mai ki'da m.s.)

A generic term which embraces all sorts of "drummers." Players of membranophones, chordophones, and idiophones are all conceived of as "drummers."

See ki'da.

maka'dan hakimai pl. (maka'din hakimai m.s.)

Equivalent of marok'an hakimai.

maka'dan sarakuna

Equivalent of marok'an sarakuna.

maka'dan Sarki

Lit. "drummers of the Emir" but used generically for all his hornblowers, acclamators, and drummers.

Equivalent of marok'an Sarki.

marok'a pl. (marok'i m.s., marok'iya f.s.)

In general, any person who acclaims another, whether solicited or not, in the hope of obtaining reward as a means of livelihood. The acclamation may be expressed in song (wak'a) or speech (kirari), with or without instrumental accompaniment, or solely on musical instruments (take).

Act of acclamation = rok'o.

karin magana:

> Rok'i rok'ak'e ka ga bak'ar rowa
> "When you beg from a marok'i you will see the worst stinginess."

marok'an baki pl.

A collective term which embraces all sorts of professional acclamators who call kirari for their patrons: e.g., San K'ira, masu kirari, 'yan ma'abba, bamba'dawa, kasken karen marok'a, and 'yan agalanda.

See marok'an baki in Part B, below, and rok'o and kirari in Section V.

marok'an hakimai or marok'an hakimi pl. (marok'in hakimi m.s.)
= masartan hakimi pl. (masarcin hakimi m.s.)
= maka'dan hakimi pl. (maka'din hakimi m.s.)

Any marok'i in the regular service of a hakimi (district head or other high official, excepting the Emir).

Instruments played by the marok'a of various hakimai of Zaria (1963-64): kakaki; algaita; gangar fada; banga; jauje; taushi; kalangun Caji; kotso; gangar algaita; kazagi; and buta.

Instruments played by the marok'a of various hakimai of Katsina (1963-65): algaita; gangar fada; gangar algaita; banga; jauje; kotso; zambuna.

See marok'an sarakuna.

marok'an sarakuna pl. (marok'in sarakuna m.s.)
= masartan sarakuna pl. (masarcin sarakuna m.s.)
= maka'dan sarakuna pl. (maka'din sarakuna m.s.)

A collective term for marok'a in the service of any high office-holder, including the Emir (the marok'an Sarki or masartan Sarki), high officials resident in

the capital of the emirate and district heads
(marok'an hakimai or masartan hakimai).

Some occasions of performance for sarakuna:

Daily -- some do rok'o in front of the patron's
residence, and in Zaria City the Sarkin Busa,
Sarkin Kakaki and Magajin Busa blow take for
the Emir and high officials in attendance.
But in Katsina the traditional unsolicited acclamation of officials, which was of daily occurrence, is now officially forbidden.

Weekly -- sara (= waza) usually on Thursday night
in front of patron's residence; escorting him
to and from the mosque on Friday; and greeting
him afterwards, called gaisuwar juma'a.

Annually -- performances during K'aramar Salla and
Babbar Salla for wazan salla, yawon salla,
hawan salla, hawan daushe and hawan kilisa.
Many accompany their patrons on his annual inspection tour.

Irregularly -- marok'an sarakuna derive considerable additional income from attendance during
the morning of naming (suna) and marriage
(aure) ceremonies, where they make announce-
ments and, if permitted, sing, drum, blow and
shout kirari. If it is their patron's ceremony, they also perform in the evening when the
feast (buki) is held. They also perform at
turbanings (na'din sarauta) of important and
affluent persons upon their investiture in office. A visit of a "V.I.P." or the return of
their patron from a long trip also require a
performance. In Zaria, the Sarkin Busa and
the Magajin Busa accompany the Emir on official business trips with the latter blowing
his trumpet from a lead automobile to herald
the Emir's coming. In Katsina, the main occasions are as above, but in addition the royal
musicians are frequently invited to perform by
various officials, within their households, on
Thursday evenings immediately after the de
rigeur sara in front of the Emir's palace.
Once a year the masu ganga, masu kotso and
masu kakaki make extended tours of the Emirate, visiting all district heads and important
village heads in the process.

marok'an <u>Sarki</u> pl. (<u>marok'in Sarki</u> m.s.)
= <u>masartan Sarki</u> pl. (<u>masarcin Sarki</u> m.s.)
= <u>maka'dan Sarki</u> pl. (<u>maka'din Sarki</u> m.s.)
= <u>maka'dan fada</u> pl. (<u>maka'din fada</u> m.s.)
= <u>marok'an fada</u> pl. (<u>marok'in fada</u> m.s.)

Any <u>marok'i</u> of an Emir including:

> heads who are given a title in recognition of
> their position and turbanned as such by an Emir;
> assistants of the heads, some of whom have lesser
> titles given them by the heads and are turbanned
> by the head. (Note: a similar pattern is encoun-
> tered among the <u>marok'an hakimi</u>.)

Titles of heads among the <u>marok'a</u> of the Emir of
Zaria in 1964 in hierarchical order:

> (i) <u>Sarkin Busa</u>; (ii) <u>Magajin Busa</u>; (iii) <u>Sarkin
> Kakaki</u>; (iv) <u>Sarkin Maka'da</u>; (v) <u>Magajin Banga</u>;
> (vi) <u>Sarkin Jauje</u>; (vii) <u>Sarkin Taushi</u>; (viii)
> <u>Sarkin Kalangu</u> ("acting"); (ix) <u>Sarkin</u> Bamba'dawa;
> (x) <u>San K'ira</u>. The head of the drummers of the
> <u>tambura</u>, the <u>Sarkin Tambari</u>, is a non-professional.

Titles of the heads of the various groups of royal
musicians at the court of the Emir of Katsina in
1965, in hierarchical order, are:

> (i) <u>Sarkin Maka'da</u>; (ii) <u>Sarkin Busa</u>; (iii) <u>Sarkin
> Maka'dan Kotso</u>; (iv) <u>Sarkin Bamba'dawa</u>; (v)
> <u>Magajin Banga</u>; (vi) <u>Sarkin Tabshi</u>; (vii) <u>Sarkin
> Farai</u>; (viii) <u>Zabaya</u>, with <u>Tambura</u>, who is outside
> the hierarchical framework.

Instruments played for the Emir of Zaria by his
<u>marok'a</u>:

> <u>k'aho</u>; <u>kakaki</u>; <u>farai</u>; <u>gangar fada</u>; <u>banga</u>; <u>jauje</u>
> and <u>kolo</u>; <u>taushi</u>; <u>kalangun Sarki</u>; and <u>kuge</u>.

Instruments used by the musicians of the Emir of
Katsina are:

> <u>tambari</u>, <u>gangar fada</u>, <u>kakaki</u>, <u>farai</u>, <u>kotso</u>,
> <u>taushi</u>, <u>banga</u>.

For occasions of performance, see <u>marok'an sarakuna</u>.

<u>masarta</u> pl. (<u>masarci</u> m.s.)

> Equivalent of <u>marok'a</u>.

masartan hakimai pl. (masarcin hakimai m.s.)
= masartan hakimi pl. (masarcin hakimi m.s.)

    Equivalent of marok'an hakimai.

masartan sarakuna pl. (masarcin sarakuna m.s.)

    Equivalent of marok'an sarakuna.

masartan Sarki pl. (masarcin Sarki m.s.)

    Term most commonly used in plural form as collective
for royal marok'a; in Zaria it includes the court
fool (wawa) and snake charmer (Sarkin Gardi), but in
Katsina is objected to by the musicians themselves,
who prefer marok'an Sarki.

    See marok'an Sarki.

masu amshi pl. (mai amshi m.s.)
= 'yan amshi pl. ('dan amshi m.s.)
= 'yan kar'bi pl. ('dan kar'bi m.s.)
= masu amsawa pl. (mai amsawa m.s.)
= 'yan amsawa pl. ('dan amsawa m.s.)

    Members of response group in singing, drumming,
trumpeting, etc.

masu kawo pl. (mai kawo m.s.)

    A synonym for all sorts of drummers of membrano-
phones. Kawo is the name of the wood (Afzelia
africana) which is commonly used to make the body-
shell of drums.

mawak'a pl. (mawak'i m.s.)
= masu wak'a pl. (mai wak'a m.s.)
= sha'irai pl. (sha'iri m.s.)

    A collective term which embraces all sorts of male
singers:

        (i) professional male singers and/or composers;
(ii) non-professional composers and/or singers of
songs; (iii) poets, though they may be distin-
guished as masu rubuta wak'a pl. (mai rubuta wak'a
m. or f.s.) or masu rubutu wak'a pl. (mai rubutu

wak'a m. or f.s.).

See wak'a.

mawak'a pl. (mawak'iya f.s.)
= zabiyoyi pl. (zabiya f.s. or zabaya f.s.)

    (i) Any female professional singer.

    (ii) Any female non-professional singer who may take
the role of the solo singer for the singing of
girls or women, but only used in connection with
her performance and not as an indicator of her
social status.

See mawak'a pl. (mawak'i m.s.)

shera m.s.

    Marok'i who dresses and acts like a woman, joining
groups of the latter in their songs and in performance of gu'da. Such activity is ridiculed by other
marok'a.

yara pl. (yaro m.s.)

    (i) Name commonly given to an apprentice musician
who is often fed, lodged and taught by the head
of his performance group.

    (ii) Name of assistant drummers and/or members of vo-
cal chorus in a performance group (e.g., yaron
Caji).

zabiyoyi pl. (zabiya f.s. or zabaya f.s.)
= marok'iya f.s.

    (i) Professional female singers.

    (ii) When married women wish to sing in their living
quarters, one of their number may be elected
"zabiya" for the singing, i.e., this woman tem-
porarily assumes the role of a lead singer but
not the social status of a professional.

See Zabiyar Sarki.

B.   CLASSES OF PERFORMERS

Introduction

Notes on the Entries

Entries will contain the following where applicable and/or where information is available:

(i) Name(s) of performers.

(ii) The letter indices opposite the names of performers are used as follows:

cm - court musicians and acclamators with official status whose patrons are Emirs, District Heads and other senior officials. Many of this class hold minor offices signified by titles (see Part C below).

t - performers without official status, but tied, like court musicians, to a distinct class of patrons, e.g., musicians of farmers, hunters or blacksmiths.

fl - performers without official status, who are freelancers.

np - semi-professionals and non-professionals who are not considered by themselves or their audiences to be marok'a.

(iii) Instrument(s) played, ensemble combinations, and description of performance role.

(iv) Patrons of performers (cross-referenced).

(v) Venue of performance, if not apparent.

(vi) Occasion(s) of performance (cross-referenced only).

(vii) Oral literature. Most entries are conventional jokes used between certain classes of performers. There are traditional joking relationships between kinsmen, ethnic groups, occupational groups and the inhabitants of different regions, people concerned in such relationships being termed abokan wasa. Here we will be concerned with an additional type: intra-occupational joking which may be termed wasa ("play") or wasan ba'a ("teasing"). Musicians tend to joke only with a class of musicians which they consider to be their equals or near-equals, and it most often takes place between drummers (maka'da) and blowers of wind instruments (masu busa).

Notes on Prefixes

The name of most kinds of performers on musical instruments may be ascertained simply by adding the prefixes mai (singular) or masu (plural) to the name of the instrument. A less common alternative is to use the following prefixes plus the genitive link "n"; mai busa or mabusa (singular) and masu busa (plural) before the names of wind instruments; and maka'di or mai ki'da (singular) and maka'da or masu ki'da (plural) before the names of most drums, string instruments and idiophones (e.g., mai busan sarewa, mai ki'dan goge, etc.).

Several instruments more often take the prefixes 'dan (singular) or 'yan (plural), e.g., 'dan kazagi and 'yan kazagi or 'dan garura and 'yan garura.

Finally, there is no reference to the instruments played in the names of certain classes of performers, chiefly professional singers (mawak'a or masu wak'a), professional acclamators (marok'an baki) and several kinds of marketplace buskers (e.g., 'yan kama).

1) Masu ki'da ("drummers")

a. Idiophonists ("Drummers on idiophones")

karen Gusau m.s. ("dog of Gusau")   fl

Musicians who play the agidigo while singing entertainment songs (wak'ar nasha'di), at naming and
marriage ceremony feasts (buki) or prior to January 1966, political songs (wak'ar siyasa) at political party gatherings (Wasan N.P.C. or
N.E.P.U.). They often play in concert with masu
kalangu and 'yan kuntuku   Audu Karen Gusau is the
best known of this comparatively small class of
performers.

masu gora pl. (mai gora m.s.)   t

Shakers of a calabash rattle (caki or gora) who
perform with masu garaya and marok'an baki for
their patrons, the 'yan bori at bori ceremonies.

They also perform with masu molo.

masu kasam'bara pl. (mai kasam'bara m.s.)   t

Idiophonists who play kasam'bara in combination
with the masu garaya and marok'an baki for their
patrons, the 'yan bori at bori ceremonies. They
are replaced in some ensemble combinations by masu
gora. Masu kasam'bara also perform with masu
molo.

masu ki'dan buta pl. (mai ki'dan buta m.s.)   t

Professional marok'a who perform especially for
Koranic scholars and teachers (malamai). They are
not to be confused with na buta. They provide
rhythmic accompaniment for their songs and dances
by shaking buta and beating them with rings on
their fingers. They also slap their leather a-
prons (buzu) rhythmically while dancing, and just
before they slap them they refer in song to the
sheepskin rug (also buzu) that malamai sit on in
their homes:

Bari mu daki buzun malan
"Let's slap the buzu of the malan."

They visit the malamai during the month of Ramadan
(watan azumi) or during one of the annual religious feasts of K'aramar Salla or Babbar Salla.

masu kuge pl. (mai kuge m.s.)   cm

(i) Beaters of the double-belled iron gong, who
play in concert with the Sarkin Kalangu of the
Emir of Zaria when there is a wazan salla, or
royal cavalcades: hawan kilisa; hawan daushe;
hawan salla. It used to be played in war-time
and in conjunction with the gangar fada, as
well as with the kalangu. Until about 20
years ago the holders of the important sarauta
titles of Madaki and Galadima owned kuge.

(ii) Beaters of kuge who play in combination with
gangar noma and kazagi of the Sarkin Maka'dan
Gangar Noma of the Emir of Zaria when playing
for the hawan salla and for buki for the general public in villages. However, kuge combined with these instruments is not common,
probably because it is viewed as an instrument
of officialdom. See marok'an sarakuna, Sarkin
Maka'da, marok'an Sarki.

'yan k'warya pl. ('dan k'warya m.s.)   fl

(i) Drummers on k'waryar goge, who play in concert
with masu goge. They are often apprentice
goge players and also act as masu amshi ("the
chorus").

(ii) Drummers on k'waryar kukuma who play in concert with masu kukuma and also act as either
mawak'i ("solo singer") or masu amshi ("the
chorus"). They are often apprentice kukuma
players.

Wasa - masu kukuma to 'yan k'waryar goge:

Mu ba mu ki'dan k'warya da itace
"We (the kukuma ensemble) don't need sticks
to beat k'warya."

See masu amada for 'yan k'warya f.pl. ('yar
k'warya f.s.)

'yan tandu pl. ('dan tandu m.s.)   fl
= masu tandu pl. (mai tandu m.s.)

Performers who beat on large, leather bottles
(tandu) while singing and doing a whirling dance
in comical costumes. Their songs are humorous,
lewd (gamtsi) and often contain zambo like those
of 'yan gambara. They perform in harlots' houses,
marketplaces or in any public place.

b. Drummers

karen marok'a ("dog of the marok'a")   t

A drummer-singer of very low rank who specializes
in rok'o for marok'a, accompanying himself on
kalangu. Dog-like, he barks in front of his patron's residence and acquires his gown by grabbing
it with his teeth. He performs for his patrons at
aure, suna, buki, tashen azumi and yawon salla.
He also attends aure, suna and buki of the general
public in the company of ordinary marok'a in order
to receive a share of their profits.

In front of his patron's house, he drums, then
barks and may sing the following:

> Wane marok'i yau rok'o ya sami rok'o
> yau rok'o gidan marok'i idan rok'o da da'di
> yau ka ta'ba shi ka ji idan ma babu da'di
>   yau ka ta'ba shi ka ji abin da kake rok'o
>   gidan wasu
> yau ga shi an zo gidanka

"You particular marok'i, today rok'o meets
rok'o, today rok'o is done at the house of
a marok'i, if rok'o is enjoyable, you will
experience it today and if it is not, all
the same you will experience it today, today is your turn to give back what you
(have received by) rok'o from other people's homes."

maka'dan mai wasa da kura pl.   f1
(maka'din mai wasa da kura m.s.)
= maka'dan gardin kura pl.
(maka'din gardin kura m.s.)

Drummers for conjurers and wrestlers of hyenas
(masu wasa da kura) who perform in the marketplace. They beat tallabe and, less often, gangar
noma with kazagi.

karin magana:

    Kura da shan bugu gardi da kar'be kur'di
    "The hyena receives the beating but his
    master receives the money."

maka'dan 'yan mata pl.   f1/t
(maka'din 'yan mata m.s.)
= masu gangar 'yan mata pl.
(mai gangar 'yan mata m.s.)

A generic term for drummers on kalangu and
kwairama or occasionally on tallabe, who are sponsored chiefly by girls ('yan mata) and older boys
and young men (samari). For performance occasions, see masu kalangu and masu kwairama. These
drummers perform in concert with 'yan kazagi, 'yan
kuntuku and marok'an baki.

maka'dan 'yan hoto pl.   t
(maka'din 'yan hoto m.s.)

Drummers on gangar noma and kazagi in accompaniment of dancing and exhibitions of strength by
'yan hoto. Performances include drumming the take
of 'yan hoto on gangar noma and singing their
praises, with the kazagi drummers acting as the
chorus (masu amshi) and vocal acclamation (kirari)
of their powers by marok'an baki.

maka'dan 'yan tauri pl.   t
(maka'din 'yan tauri m.s.)
= masu ki'dan kufegere pl.
(mai ki'dan kufegere m.s.)

Praise singers and drummers of take on talle and
sometimes on kalangu or gangar noma, who play only
for their fellow 'yan tauri and do not consider
themselves to be marok'a, though they receive

payment for playing for their <u>wasan</u> <u>'yan</u> <u>tauri</u>, <u>buki</u> and <u>na'din</u> <u>sarauta</u>. They also march annually in the <u>hawan</u> <u>salla</u> parade and special parades for V.I.P. (<u>daba</u>). Since many <u>'yan</u> <u>tauri</u> are butchers, they perform at the butchers' boxing matches (<u>dambe</u>), turbannings (<u>na'din</u> <u>sarauta</u>) and drum in the market (<u>ki'dan</u> <u>mahauta</u>) for them before feast days.

<u>Wasa</u> - <u>masu</u> <u>talle</u> to <u>Malamai</u>:

<u>Zo</u> <u>ka</u> 'dauki <u>ganga</u> <u>ka</u> <u>aje</u> <u>alk'alami</u>
"Come and take the drum and put down the pen."

<u>Malamai</u> reply:

<u>Za</u> <u>ka</u> 'dauki <u>alk'alami</u> <u>da</u> <u>takarda</u> <u>ka</u> <u>bar</u> <u>ganga</u>?
"Will you take the pen and paper and leave the drum?"

<u>masu</u> <u>banga</u> pl. (<u>mai</u> <u>banga</u> m.s.)   cm

Drummers on <u>banga</u> for an Emir or a senior official, who sing songs in praise (<u>wak'ar</u> <u>yabo</u>) of their patron or his associates. In Katsina and Zaria, the head of the ensemble (<u>Magajin</u> <u>Banga</u>) is the song leader (<u>mawak'i</u>), and the assistant drummers, some of whom hold lesser titles, act as chorus (<u>masu</u> <u>amshi</u>). See <u>marok'an</u> <u>sarakuna</u> for performance occasions. See also <u>marok'an</u> <u>Sarki</u>.

<u>Wasa</u> - <u>masu</u> <u>algaita</u> to <u>masu</u> <u>banga</u>:

<u>Sai</u> <u>mun</u> <u>ga</u> <u>abin</u> <u>da</u> <u>kuke</u> <u>rufewa</u> <u>da</u> <u>wannan</u> <u>tsumma</u> <u>haka</u>
"We must see what you are covering with the rags."

<u>masu</u> <u>kotso</u> to <u>masu</u> <u>banga</u>:

<u>Mu</u> <u>ya'ya</u> <u>ne</u> <u>kullun</u> <u>muna</u> <u>gaba</u> <u>ku</u> <u>kuwa</u> <u>an</u> <u>tura</u> <u>ku</u> <u>baya</u>
"We are small children, always at the head of the procession -- while you are pushed to the rear*." (* reference to their traditional place in royal processions)

<u>masu</u> <u>banga</u> replies:

Mu <u>mun</u> <u>fiku</u> <u>gatanci</u> <u>tunda</u> mu <u>ana</u> <u>goyonmu</u> <u>ku</u>
<u>kuwa</u> <u>sai</u> a <u>tura</u> <u>ku</u> <u>gaba</u> <u>ku</u> <u>kai</u> ma <u>zuma</u>
<u>gidanta</u>
"We are more favoured than you because we
are always protected at the back while you
are pushed forward to the hive* of the
bees." (* reference to the drums they
carry)

<u>masu</u> <u>kotso</u> to <u>masu</u> <u>banga</u>:

Ku <u>kai</u> ma <u>mai</u> <u>kalangu</u> <u>kuntukunshi</u>
"Return the <u>kuntuku</u>* to its owner, <u>mai</u>
<u>kalangu</u>." (* It looks like the <u>banga</u> but
it is played by apprentices of low-ranking
<u>kalangu</u> drummers.)

<u>masu</u> <u>duma</u> pl. (<u>mai</u> <u>duma</u> m.s.)   fl

Singers and drummers on <u>duma</u>.

<u>karin</u> <u>magana</u>:

> 'Dan <u>kazagi</u> <u>ya</u> <u>fi</u> <u>mai</u> <u>duma</u> 'doki
> "The performer on <u>kazagi</u> surpasses the per-
> former on <u>duma</u> in his eagerness," i.e., it
> is the lesser member of a partnership who
> is the keenest.

<u>masu</u> <u>duman</u> <u>girke</u> pl.
(<u>mai</u> <u>duman</u> <u>girke</u> m.s.)

Singers and drummers on <u>duman</u> <u>girke</u>.

<u>masu</u> <u>gangar</u> <u>algaita</u> pl.   cm
(<u>mai</u> <u>gangar</u> <u>algaita</u> m.s.)

Singers and drummers on <u>gangar</u> <u>algaita</u> for a senior official, who play in ensemble with <u>masu</u>
<u>algaita</u> in honour of their patron or his associ-
ates. The head of these drummers, as well as of
the blowers of <u>algaita</u>, is usually the lead singer
and given the title and office of <u>Sarkin</u> <u>Maka'da</u>.
The other drummers act as the chorus (<u>masu</u> <u>amshi</u>)
and some hold the lesser titles of <u>Madakin</u> <u>Ki'da</u>,
<u>Makaman</u> <u>Ki'da</u>, and <u>Wazirin</u> <u>Ganga</u>. For occasions
of performance see <u>marok'an</u> <u>sarakuna</u>.

masu gangar noma pl.   t
(mai gangar noma m.s.)

    Drummers of gangar noma, commonly encountered in
Zaria, but rare in Katsina, who recognize farmers
(manoma) as their traditional and primary patrons,
though some -- Sarkin Maka'dan Gangar Noma -- play
also for sarakuna or the performances of 'yan hoto
and gardin kura. They drum a farmer's take at co-
operative group work (gayya) and sing his praise
(wak'ar yabo) at feasts (buki), with 'yan kazagi
acting as the chorus (masu amshi) and the marok'an
baki shouting their kirari. Masu gangar noma also
perform at kalankuwa and rawan Cane. They used to
drum regularly for girls' dancing (rawan 'yan mata)
in rural communities but the masu kalangu and masu
kwairama have, for the most part, replaced them in
this role.

Wasa - masu gangar noma to masu busa (or kakaki
     or farai):

    Masu abu da tsawo
    "You are the owners of the long thing."

    masu busa replies:

    Masu 'dauke da kayan nauyi ko da yaushe
    a wuyansu
    "You are the one who carries the heavy load
    always around his neck."

masu gangar fada pl.   cm
(mai gangar fada m.s.)
= masu gangar saraki pl.
(mai gangar saraki m.s.)

    Drummers on gangar fada for an Emir or a senior
official, who play in his honour the take of his
office and either sing (wak'ar yabo) or call
(kirari) his praises. The vocalist (mawak'i), if
any, is the head of the ensemble (Sarkin Maka'da)
and the other drummers, on some occasions, are the
chorus (masu amshi). The masu gangar fada perform
in a variety of ensembles. They play with a mai
algaita (masu algaita) for the District Head of
Kauru in Zaria, but they play alone for the District Head of Kajuru. The masu gangar fada of the
Emir of Zaria combine in performance with masu
k'aho, masu farai, masu kakaki, the royal
bamba'dawa and the San K'ira and his marok'an baki

assistants. For the Emir of Katsina, the masu
gangar fada perform with masu kakaki and masu
farai. See marok'an sarakuna for performance occasions.

Wasa - masu k'aho to masu gangar fada:

Kun 'dauko gidan zuma
"You carry around a beehive!"

masu jauje pl. (mai jauje m.s.)   cm

Drummers on jauje and kolo for officialdom, who
sing songs of praise (wak'ar yabo) and drum the
take of their patron or his associates. The head
of the ensemble (Sarkin Jauje) is the song leader
(mawak'i), and the assistant drummers, some of
whom have lesser titles, are the chorus (masu
amshi). For performance occasions see marok'an
sarakuna. See also marok'an Sarki.

Wasa - masu busa (or any player of an aerophone
for the Emir) to masu jauje:

Yaya kuka ji da tsarkiya da ta ke kama ku
a hak'ark'ari
"How do you feel when the tsarkiya grabs
your ribs?"

masu jauje replies:

Ku cikin ku ban da iska ba komai
"There is nothing in your stomach except
air."

masu busa to masu jauje:

Kuna 'dauke da gidan zuma
"You are carrying a beehive."

masu kalangu pl. (mai kalangu m.s.)   t/fl
= masu ki'dan kalangu pl.
(mai ki'dan kalangu m.s.)

A very large class of drummers who perform on
kalangu for: (i) butchers (mahauta), their traditional patrons; (ii) the youth (samari and 'yan
mata); (iii) the general public, in the case of
those who play in the bands of popular freelance
singers, such as Alhaji Muhamman Shata.

(i) Butchers: they drum their patron's take for naming and marriage feasts (buki), turbannings (na'din sarauta) and evening visitations during the month of Ramadan (tashen azumi). They drum (ki'dan fawa) to announce market slaughtering and to attract customers for their patrons, and as an accompaniment to playing with bulls (wasan hawan k'aho) to encourage the sale of meat before a feast day, such as Sallar Cika Ciki. They also drum the take of boxers ('yan dambe), who are usually butchers.

(ii) Youth: the kalangu/'dan kar'bi drum set plus one or more kuntuku is used for youths' dancing, plays, ceremonies and sports. The kuntuku are played by 'yan kuntuku and the performing group also normally includes one or more marok'an baki. Usually in connection with buki they accompany the girls' dancing (rawan 'yan mata) and singing (wak'ar 'yan mata), and drum the take of both the girls and the young men at the dancing place. They also perform for kai gara and ajo for marriages, boxing (dambe), dancing of boys and young men (a sha k'afa) and various plays of the youth (wasan misisi and kwanta).

(iii) The general public: as above.

For other uses see Caji, 'yan gambara, masu kalangun Sarki, k'aramar kalangu and kalangun Sarki.

Wasa - masu goge to masu kalangu:

Ku sai 'yan mata kuna ta buge-buge suna jefa maku kwabo
"You only play for the girls to dance and give you pennies."

masu kalangu replies:

Ku sai karuwai suna maku rawa suna jefa taba ku k'arasa
"You only play for the harlots to dance and give you a half-smoked cigarette to finish up."

masu kalangun Sarki pl.   cm
(mai kalangun Sarki m.s.)

Drummers on kalangun Sarki and kolo, who drum take
in honour of the Emir or his associates. They also occasionally perform in combination with a
player of a double iron bell (masu kuge). For occasions of performance see marok'an sarakuna; however, they do not perform each week (waza) at the
palace of the Emir of Zaria, as the other court
musicians do.

masu kotso pl. (mai kotso m.s.)   cm

Drummers on kotso for officialdom, who sing songs
of praise (wak'ar yabo) and drum take for their
patrons or their patrons' associates. The head of
the ensemble (Magajin Kotso in Zaria; in Katsina,
Sarkin Maka'dan Kotso) is the lead singer
(mawak'i), and the assistant drummers, some of
whom have lesser titles, are the chorus (masu
amshi). For performance occasions see marok'an
sarakuna.

Wasa - masu algaita to masu kotso:

   Ku cire daddawan tsohuwa da kuka namma
   a jiki
   "Remove the locust bean cake* that you
   stick on your bodies (drums)." (* The
   locust bean cake stands for the nake on
   the membrane.)

masu kuru pl. (mai kuru m.s.)

As for masu gangar noma.

masu kurya pl. (mai kurya m.s.)   cm

Drummers on kurya for an official of an Emir who
perform take in honour of their patron or his associates (e.g., in Katsina by the musicians of
Sarkin Karma who, himself the official of a district head, was traditionally in charge of the
latter's infantry). In performance they may combine with one or more other masu kurya and masu
kalangu, though the drum is more commonly used
singly with kalangu, the main occasions being marriage and naming ceremonies of their patron and

his family, and major festivals such as Babbar
Salla and K'aramar Salla; they also drummed formerly in time of war to assemble the infantry and
lead them into battle (see kirarin kurya, in Section I). The drum is also used by non-official
freelance musicians in combination with duma and
kazagi.

masu kwairama pl.   fl
(mai kwairama m.s.)
= maka'dan 'yan mata pl.
(maka'din 'yan mata m.s.)
= masu gangar 'yan mata pl.
(mai gangar 'yan mata m.s.)

Drummers on kwairama in Zaria who perform solo or
in combination with other masu kwairama and one or
more 'yan kazagi, for the youth ('yan mata and
samari). More often found in rural communities
than in the cities, and in the former masu kalangu
appear to be gradually superseding them. Some occasions in which they perform are rawan 'yan mata,
buki, kai gara, kalankuwa, rawan Gane, a sha k'afa
and kokawa. They drum the take of the youth and
sing a variety of songs (wak'ar nasha'di, wak'ar
yabo and wak'ar abayyana).

masu taushi pl. (mai taushi m.s.)   cm
= masu tabshi pl. (mai tabshi m.s.)

Singers and drummers on taushi for officialdom,
who perform songs in praise (wak'ar yabo) of their
patron or his associates. In Zaria and Katsina,
the head of the ensemble (Sarkin Taushi) is the
song leader (mawak'i) and the assistant drummers,
some of whom have lesser titles, are the chorus
(masu amshi). In Katsina, the chief taushi drummer for the Emir, Sarkin Tabshin Katsina Alhaji
Mamman, is known throughout Hausaland for his
songs in praise of individuals and on national
topics. For performance occasions, see marok'an
sarakuna. See also marok'an Sarki.

masu tallabe pl. (mai tallabe m.s.)   fl

Drummers on tallabe, who perform with 'yan gambara,
na uwale and masu wasa da kura. A few have been
observed drumming for the singing and dancing of
the youth (samari and 'yan mata). Professional

tattoers ('yan jarfa) also use tallabe or smaller
double-membraned drums like gangar algaita.

masu zambuna pl. (mai zambuna f.s.)   cm

Singers and drummers on zambuna unique to the office of Mara'din Kurfi in Katsina Emirate. Occasions and venues of performance are as for
marok'an sarakuna.

'yan dundufa pl. ('dan dundufa m.s.)   t
= masu dundufa pl. (mai dundufa m.s.)

Singers and drummers on dundufa who sing praise
songs (wak'ar yabo) in honour of their traditional
patrons, the blacksmiths (mak'era), on such occasions as buki or na'din sarauta. They also greet
the chief of their patrons, the Sarkin Mak'era,
each Friday after prayers at the mosque (gaisuwar
juma'a). There was only one family of 'yan
dundufa performing in the emirate of Zaria in
1963-64, but at least four in Katsina Emirate in
the same period.

'yan kashin kasuwa = 'yan yabo   fl

Persons who defecate in public or threaten to do
so unless paid. They perform mainly in markets to
musical accompaniment, kalangu or tallabe, and
kazagi.

'yan kazagi pl. ('dan kazagi m.s.)   fl/t

Young men or boys, who can most often be found
drumming kazagi in concert with masu gangar noma
or masu kwairama, and singing the chorus refrains.
They also perform with mawak'an Caji, 'yan gambara,
masu wasa da kura, 'yan kashin kasuwa, and 'yan
dundufa. They play the kazagi and perform as masu
amshi while learning to play gangar noma, kwairama,
and dundufa.

'yan kuntuku pl. ('dan kuntuku m.s.)   t
= masu kurkutu pl. (mai kurkutu m.s.)

Boy drummers on kuntuku (kurkutu), who perform
with masu kalangu for youths' dancing, ceremonies

and games, as well as in the bands of such famous musicians as Alhaji Muhamman Shata, Ali 'Dan Saraki, etc. Young apprentices often play the kuntuku while learning to play the kalangu.

'yan tagaba pl. ('dan tagaba m.s.)   fl
= masu rok'o da kuka pl.
(mai rok'o da kuka m.s.)

Professional cadgers who say "If you don't give me something I'll cry" and tell exceedingly sad, hard-luck stories. They accompany themselves on kalangu and are usually found in the market place. Non-professional cadgers who do not drum with their "performance" may also be referred to by the same term.

yaran Caji pl. (yaron Caji m.s.)   fl

Members of a Caji performance group under a leader and singer such as the famous Hamza Caji or Ibrahim 'Dan Mani Caji. As such, they act as both drummer on gangar Caji, kazagi or k'aramar kalangu, and as member of the vocal chorus (masu amshi).

c. Lutenists ("Drummers on chordophones")

masu garaya pl. (mai garaya m.s.)   t/fl

Any performers on garaya, the instrument which was originally played in honour of hunters, but today, in view of the decrease in the numbers of the lat- ter, is increasingly used for other types of music (see kirarin mai garaya, below). Those who per- form for hunters in Zaria, play the large garaya (komo or babbar garaya) and prefer to be called masu komo, though the general public does not make this distinction. Performers on the garaya -- usually the smaller type -- may also accompany spirit possession dancers at bori ceremonies, which are normally held in harlots' houses. Masu garayar bori, as such specialists are called, also sing songs in praise of bori spirits (wak'ar bori) and of some of the spectators. They perform with one or more masu gora or masu kasam'bara and one or more marok'an baki. Masu garayar bori may also

play for _buki_ and some have become freelance musicians who perform _wak'ar_ _nasha'di_ for the general
public.

kirarin _mai_ _garaya_ (_kirari_ for a _garaya_ player):

> _Inda_ _ba_ _mahalbi_ _mai_ _garaya_ _ma_ _mahalbi_ _ne_
> "When there is no hunter, the _garaya_ player
> becomes the hunter (for patronage)."

Wasa - _masu_ _goge_ to _masu_ _garaya_:

> _Za_ _mu_ _yi_ _k'aran_ _ku_ _wajen_ _Maguzawa_ _sabo_ _da_
> _kun_ _hana_ _musu_ _cin_ _fatan_ _gafiya_ _kun_ _'dauka_
> _kun_ _dunka_ _garaya_ _da_ _shi_
> "We shall report you to the Maguzawa (pagan
> Hausa), because you have prevented them
> from eating the skin of the bandicoot by
> using it to make _garaya_."

Wasa - _masu_ _kukuma_ to _masu_ _garayar_ _bori_:

> _Mu_ _namu_ _ki'dan_ _ba_ _ma_ _yin_ _ki'dan_ _bori_ _da_
> _shi_ _balle_ _a_ _yi_ _rawa_
> "As for our drumming, it's certainly not
> for _bori_ let alone dancing."

masu _garaya_ reply:

> _Ai_ _mu_ _namu_ _tsarkiyar_ _biyu_ _ne_ _don_ _haka_ _muke_
> _ki'dan_ _bori_ _da_ _shi_ _a_ _yi_ _ta_ _nisha'di_
> "Ours always has two strings and that is
> why we do _bori_ drumming and give so much
> pleasure."

masu _goge_ pl. (_mai_ _goge_ m.s.)   fl

Performer on _goge_ in concert with _'yan_ _k'waryar_
goge and _marok'an_ _baki_ for the following occasions
and patrons: (i) the activities of political parties (_wasan_ N.P.C. or N.E.P.U. and _rawan_ _kashewa_)
until January 1966. See _wak'ar_ _siyasa_; (ii) prom-
inent persons, whether members of officialdom,
politicians, or wealthy merchants. See _wak'ar_
yabo; (iii) _'yan_ _bori_ for _bori_ ceremonies. See
wak'ar _bori_; (iv) _ajo_ ceremonies to raise money,
normally to help the bridegroom meet marriage expenses; (v) the dancing of harlots and praise in
song (_wak'ar_ _yabo_) and speech (_kirari_) of harlots
and their patrons.

<u>Wasa</u> - <u>masu garaya</u> to <u>masu goge</u>:

<u>Za mu kar'be gogenku mu ba zuma ya yi sak'a
a ciki</u>
"We will seize your <u>goge</u> and give it to the
bees to put their hive in." (Note: reference to hole in calabash resonator like
hole in beehive.)

<u>masu garaya</u> to <u>masu goge</u>:

<u>Adabo-adabo</u>* <u>mai goge ya ga farkansa</u>
(* <u>adabo</u> d.f. Yoruba <u>odabo</u>)
"Good-bye, good-bye, <u>mai goge</u> sees his
girlfriend."

<u>masu gurmi</u> pl. (<u>mai gurmi</u> m.s.)

Performers on <u>gurmi</u> who traditionally played and
sang in honour of <u>'yan kokuwa</u>, but are today a
vanishing class of musician.

<u>masu komo</u> pl. (<u>mai komo</u> m.s.)   t

Performing solo or in a group they sing praise
songs (<u>wak'ar yabo</u>) for their traditional patrons,
the hunters (<u>maharba</u>), accompanying themselves on
the lute (<u>komo</u> or <u>babbar garaya</u>). They perform
for hunters' feasts (<u>buki</u>), turbannings (<u>na'din
sarauta</u>), big hunts (<u>bago</u>), and they march with
their patrons in the annual feast-day processions
(<u>hawan salla</u> and <u>hawan daushe</u>).

<u>Wasa</u> - <u>masu gangar noma</u> to <u>masu komo</u>:

<u>Ku lik'e wannan ramin, mu gani ko ya
yi k'ara</u>
"Block up that hole (in your <u>komo</u>) and
let's see if it still wails."

<u>masu komo</u> reply:

<u>Ku kwance tsarkiyar ku buga mu gani in
zai yi k'ara</u>
"Loosen your <u>tsarkiya</u> and drum and let's
see if it will still wail."

See <u>masu garaya</u>.

<u>masu</u> <u>kukuma</u> pl. (<u>mai</u> <u>kukuma</u> m.s.)   fl/np

<u>Marok'a</u> who perform on <u>kukuma</u> and/or sing (<u>wak'ar</u>
<u>nasha'di</u>, <u>wak'ar yabo</u>, <u>wak'ar siyasa</u> and <u>bege</u>) for
the general public in combination with '<u>yan</u>
<u>k'warya</u>, who beat <u>k'waryar</u> <u>kukuma</u>. They most often
perform for wealthy merchants (<u>attajirai</u>), officialdom (<u>sarakuna</u>), and for harlots and their patrons. Some also perform at political party func-
tions, <u>ajo</u>, <u>buki</u> and <u>kalankuwa</u> celebrations. Non-
<u>marok'a</u> (young men and women, and married women)
also play <u>kukuma</u> for pleasure.

<u>Wasa</u> - <u>masu</u> <u>kukuma</u> to <u>masu</u> <u>goge</u>:

> <u>Kukuma</u> <u>ba</u> <u>ta</u> <u>kukan</u> <u>kura</u> <u>ba</u> <u>ta</u> <u>kukan</u> <u>jaki</u>
> "The <u>kukuma</u> does not cry like a hyena but
> like a jackass."

<u>masu</u> <u>kukuma</u> to '<u>yan</u> <u>kuntigi</u>:

> <u>Naku</u> <u>ba</u> <u>shi</u> <u>da</u> <u>k'ara</u> <u>kamar</u> <u>namar</u> <u>namu</u> <u>dom</u>
> <u>ba</u> <u>za'a</u> <u>ji</u> <u>a</u> <u>nesa</u> <u>ba</u>
> "Yours doesn't wail with a body of sound
> like ours because it can't be heard from
> afar."

'<u>yan</u> <u>kuntigi</u> reply:

> <u>Mu</u> <u>namu</u> <u>ko</u> <u>a</u> <u>ina</u> <u>ya</u> <u>kama</u> <u>sai</u> <u>mu</u> <u>yi</u> <u>don</u>
> <u>a</u> <u>aljihu</u> <u>muke</u> <u>tafe</u> <u>da</u> <u>shi</u>
> "Ours can be played anywhere because we
> carry it in our pocket."

<u>masu</u> <u>molo</u> pl. (<u>mai</u> <u>molo</u> m.s.)   fl/np

Male singers of songs of entertainment and praise
(<u>wak'ar</u> <u>nasha'di</u> and <u>wak'ar</u> <u>yabo</u>) who accompany
themselves on the three-stringed plucked lute
(<u>molo</u>). They perform solo or in combination with
<u>masu</u> <u>kasam'bara</u> or <u>masu</u> <u>gora</u> for the general pub-
lic and for harlots and their patrons. Like the
<u>kukuma</u> and <u>kuntigi</u>, the <u>molo</u> is also played by
non-professionals for their own pleasure.

'<u>yan</u> <u>kuntigi</u> pl. ('<u>dan</u> <u>kuntigi</u> m.s.)   fl/np

Male or, less often, female solo singers of various types of song, e.g., songs of entertainment
(<u>wak'ar</u> <u>nasha'di</u>), political songs (<u>wak'ar</u> <u>siyasa</u>),

and praise songs (wak'ar yabo), who accompany
themselves on a single-stringed plucked lute
(kuntigi). Made popular as an accompaniment instrument by the artistry of such singers as 'Dan
Maraya and Mai Kur'di 'Dan Duna. Such performers
play for wedding and naming feasts (buki) of
Emirs, senior officials and wealthy merchants,
and, prior to January 1966, entertained at political party gatherings (wasan N.P.C. or N.E.P.U.).
Other performers play more often for lorry drivers
in carparks, gamblers and harlots. Like the
kukuma and the molo, the kuntigi is also played by
non-professionals for their own pleasure.

Wasa - Caji singer to 'yan kuntigi:

Mu ba mu yin ki'dan gwangwani
"We are not playing a small tin can."

'yan kuntigi reply:

Mu ba ruwanmu da kwaramniya
"We are not concerned with so much noise."

2) Masu busa ("blowers")

masu algaita pl. (mai algaita m.s.)   cm

Blowers of the double reed pipe (algaita) of a
senior official but not of the Emir in Katsina and
Zaria. Solo or in ensemble, take are performed in
honour of the official, which are normally synchronized with songs of praise (wak'ar yabo) sung
by the leader of the group, the Sarkin Maka'da and
his chorus, the masu gangar algaita. Senior players of the algaita often hold the title and office
of Magajin Busa and assistant algaita players
sometimes have lesser titles. Masu algaita also
perform in combination with masu kakaki, masu
farai and masu gangar fada. For performance occasions see marok'an sarakuna.

Wasa - masu kotso to masu algaita:

Za mu zo mu rik'e hancinku mu ga ta inda
za ku yi numfashi

"We will come and squeeze your nose and
then see if you will breathe." (Said when
algaita is blowing.)

masu banga to masu algaita:

Ku ba mu bututunmu za mu je mu ba doki
magani (and tries to grab the algaita)
"Give us our funnel (algaita), we are going
to give medicine to the horse."

masu algaita to maka'dan Sarki:

Kuna tafe da kaya
"You travel with a load."

maka'dan Sarki replies:

Ba sai mun nemi ruwa ba
"We don't always search for water."

masu busan til'boro pl.   np/fl
(mai busan til'boro m.s.)

Young men who blow til'boro for their peers in accompaniment of dance, acclamation and song. They
perform after the farming season and during watan
azumi. They are semi-professional and are not
considered marok'a. Others, particularly small
boys, blow til'boro solely for their own amusement.

masu farai pl. (mai farai m.s.)   cm

Blowers of wooden lip-vibrated trumpet (farai) of
the Emirs of Zaria and Katsina, though in Zaria,
in former times, high officials with titles of
Waziri and Madaki had masu farai of their own; in
Katsina, however, the instrument appears to be of
comparatively recent introduction. Masu farai
perform in combination with masu k'aho, masu
kakaki and masu gangar fada, and they more or less
synchronize the take they blow with those played
by the other musicians at, for example, a fanfare
(waza) performed in honour of their patron every
Thursday evening. In Katsina, the head of the
masu farai has the title and office of Sarkin
Farai, but in Zaria he is called the Magajin Busa
and is number two in the rank hierarchy. The
Magajin Busa performs solo daily in front of the
Emir's palace, blowing the take and sometimes

shouting the <u>kirari</u> of approaching officials to
notify the Emir of their arrival, and he accompa-
nies the Emir on official business trips by auto,
blowing his trumpet to notify the people of the
Emir's arrival. For additional performance occasions, see <u>marok'an</u> <u>sarakuna</u>.

<u>Wasa</u> - <u>masu</u> <u>gangar</u> <u>noma</u> to <u>masu</u> <u>farai</u>:

> <u>Me</u> <u>ya</u> <u>sa</u> <u>ba</u> <u>ku</u> <u>hurawa</u> <u>ba</u> <u>tare</u> <u>da</u> <u>kun</u> <u>sa</u>
> <u>ruwa</u> <u>ba?</u> <u>Kuna</u> <u>'dauke</u> <u>da</u> <u>kwarkwaro</u> <u>ne?</u>
> "Why is it you don't blow unless you've
> poured water? Are you carrying a funnel?"

<u>masu</u> <u>farai</u> replies:

> <u>Ku</u> <u>kuma</u> <u>mu</u> <u>zuba</u> <u>k'asa</u> <u>mu</u> <u>ga</u> <u>wanda</u> <u>zai</u>
> <u>iya</u> <u>'dauka</u>
> "As for you, let's fill our instruments
> with sand and see who can carry it."

<u>masu</u> <u>k'aho</u> pl. (<u>mai</u> <u>k'aho</u> m.s.)   cm/fl

(i) Blowers of the side-blown, roan antelope
horn (<u>k'aho</u>) of the Emir of Zaria. In former times the <u>Waziri</u> of Zaria, second in
rank to the Emir, and the <u>Fagaci</u>, a District Head, had <u>masu</u> <u>k'aho</u> of their own.
The head of the royal musicians, the <u>Sarkin</u>
<u>Busa</u>, blows the <u>k'aho</u> and as the Emir's
chief musician, he is considered the head
of all of the musicians of the emirate.
The <u>Sarkin</u> <u>Busa</u> performs solo daily in
front of the Emir's Council Chamber, blowing the <u>take</u> of each approaching senior official to notify the Emir of the arrival.
He performs with one or more <u>masu</u> <u>k'aho</u> in
concert with <u>masu</u> <u>kakaki</u>, <u>masu</u> <u>farai</u> and
<u>masu</u> <u>gangar</u> <u>fada</u> for royal fanfares in hon-
our of the Emir held, for example, on
Thursday evenings (<u>waza</u>). On these occasions the <u>take</u> played by each class of performers is more or less synchronized with
those blown by the <u>masu</u> <u>k'aho</u>. For other
occasions of performance see <u>marok'an</u>
<u>sarakuna</u>.

(ii) A smaller horn of a gazelle (<u>k'ahon</u> <u>tsauri</u>)
is blown by non-official professional musi-
cians in rural communities for such occa-
sions as <u>kalankuwa</u>, <u>wasan</u> <u>'yan</u> <u>tauri</u>, and

rawan Gane. They perform together with
masu gangar noma and 'yan kazagi.

It should be noted that the wawa, the court fool,
of the Emir of Zaria carries a large k'aho like
that of the Sarkin Busa, but he does not play more
than one tone on it or attempt to play take, i.e.,
he simply toots it once or twice when the Emir
makes an appearance.

Wasa - Sarkin Maka'da to Sarkin Busa:

Ka 'dauko k'ahon sa ne?
"You are bringing an ox horn?"

masu gangar fada to masu k'aho:

Ba ku zuwa gari sai da k'uk'umi
"You never enter a town unless you are tied
(like a slave or prisoner)."* (* a reference to the playing position of the masu
k'aho)

masu kakaki pl. (mai kakaki m.s.)   cm

Blowers of the long metal trumpet (kakaki) of an
Emir and more rarely, as in Zaria, of a few senior
officials: the Galadiman Zazzau and the Sarkin
Kauru. In Katsina the previous Emir, Alhaji
Muhamman Dikko, gave a kakaki to Sarkin Musawa, a
District Head of whom he was very fond, but such
an action has never since been repeated. In Zaria
the head of the masu kakaki holds the title and
office of Sarkin Kakaki, in Katsina he holds the
title and office of Sarkin Busa, while in both
places some of the others have lesser titles. He
blows the take of his patron's office, solo or
with one or more masu kakaki in a leader and chorus response style. Different combinations of the
following perform with masu kakaki: masu farai;
masu k'aho; masu gangar fada; bamba'dawa; and the
royal marok'an baki. In general, the most frequent occasion for their use is the weekly sara
(= waza) on Thursday evenings, other occasions being the turbanning of officials and, in Katsina,
performances solicited by an official after the
weekly sara. Uniquely, perhaps, the Sarkin Kakaki
of the Emir of Zaria performs solo with the royal
tambura from time to time and every morning at
dawn he climbs up on a rock outcrop near the palace and blows take honouring his patron and

greeting the people at the beginning of a new day.
For other occasions of performance see marok'an
sarakuna.

Wasa - masu gangar fada to masu kakaki:

Abinka da tsawo
"Your thing is very long!"

masu kakaki to masu gangar fada:

Ai arziki ne?
"Surely it is wealth?"

masu kakaki to the maka'da:

Idan ana ruwa kowa ya fita da kayan
sana'anshi mu ga wanda zai jik'e
"When it is raining and everyone goes out
with the tools of his trade, we will see
which one gets soaked."

masu jauje to masu kakaki:

Kuna tafe da dogon gwangwala na zunguro
dabino
"You are carrying a stick for knocking down
date nuts."

masu sarewa pl.   np/fl
(mai sarewa m.s.)

Blowers of sarewa, both professionals and non-
professionals.

'yan damalgo   np/fl
('dan damalgo m.s.)
= masu busan damalgo pl.
(mai busan damalgo m.s.)

Damalgo blowers, singers and dancers who perform
in the streets during the month of Ramadan (watan
azumi) for the general public. They are semi-
professionals who receive a little money for performing, but are not considered marok'a.

3) Mawak'a ("singers")

masu amada pl. (mai amada m.s.)   fl
= mawak'an amada pl.
(mawak'in amada m.s.)

Professional female singers (zabiya) who perform
especially for women at buki in the women's quarters. Songs (wak'ar nasha'di, wak'ar siyasa and
wak'ar yabo) are sung in the amada style (ki'dan
amada), a singer either accompanying herself on a
calabash drum (k'warya) or a set of calabash drums
(k'waryar ki'dan ruwa) played by the singer and
her chorus ('yan k'warya f.pl., 'yar k'warya f.s.).
Songs ridiculing co-wives are especially popular
(wak'ar kishiya). The 'yan k'warya are either
professionals or non-professionals, usually the
latter.

mawak'an bege pl.   cm/np
(mawak'in bege m.s.)

Professional unaccompanied "singers" of religious
poems nostalgically praising the Prophet (see bege
and wak'a). It should be noted that there is a
separate class of blind beggars who similarly
praise the Prophet but are not viewed as marok'a.
They are thought to bring good fortune to their
donors and some, like Malan Aliyu Namangi of Zaria,
have become revered poets and scholars, who are
called masu bege. Malan Aliyu has set some of his
religious poems to Caji drum rhythms and performs
them over the radio.

mawak'an Caji pl.   fl
(mawak'in Caji m.s.)

Popular singers and heads of bands which play the
Caji style of music, which was originated by Hamza
Caji of Kano. Caji singers, known for the clever
lyrics of their songs (wak'ar nasha'di and wak'ar
yabo) and their style of drumming (ki'dan Caji),
travel much of the time with their bands, playing
especially for officialdom (sarakuna) and wealthy
merchants (attajirai), on such occasions as buki,
tashen azumi and yawon salla. The instruments

used in Caji bands are the gangar Caji, kalangu
and kazagi and they are performed upon by yaron
Caji, who also perform as the vocal chorus.

mawak'an kukuma pl.   fl
(mawak'in kukuma m.s.)

Lead singers and often the heads of kukuma bands
who may or may not play the kukuma. See masu
kukuma for patrons and performance occasions.

mawak'an Hamisu pl.   fl/cm
(mawak'in Hamisu m.s.)

Singers in Hamisu style who accompany themselves
on ganga, in combination with one or more players
of ganga and kazagi, who sing the vocal responses.
Mawak'an Hamisu sing wak'ar yabo and wak'ar
nasha'di for the general public, especially for
attajirai and other wealthy persons. In Zaria,
one such singer and his band are court musicians
of a District Head. The Hamisu style was made
popular by the artistry of Hamisu Na Biyar.

mawak'an Shata pl.

Professional male singers who imitate the style
and voice quality of Alhaji Muhamman Shata, the
most famous and successful of all present-day
singers. The term is, however, frequently used
derogatively, implying the singer has no talent of
his own.

mawak'an 'yan mata pl.   fl
(mawak'in 'yan mata m.s.)

Several male professional singers in Zaria City
who are the song leaders of the girls' chorus,
singing in a falsetto voice and dancing from time
to time, to rhythms of kalangu, 'dan kar'bi and
kuntuku. They are in demand for such occasions as
buki, wasan misisi and kwanta. They also do
tashen azumi and sing wak'ar abayyana for the annual rawan Gane. See masu kalangu.

na uwale   fl

Professional comedians who sing (wak'ar gamtsi)
and/or talk and dance humorously and lewdly in
marketplaces, stripped to the waist and dressed in
huge baggy trousers (buje) and long red hats
(dara). Others paint their faces blue or with
charcoal and wear enormous turbans and ride don-
keys in turbanning processions. They do acrobatics, imitations (e.g., of 'yan tauri) and make
funny faces. They are accompanied by marok'a
playing tallabe, kalangu, kazagi or damalgo. Have
been observed performing with 'yan gambara. See
'yan kama.

'yan daji pl. ('dan daji m.s.)   fl

Do tashe during watan azumi, dressed in gowns made
of old mats with many pieces of metal and calabash
attached to them. Sing and dance humorously, providing own rhythmic accompaniment by beating ruwan
gatari against ruwan patenya.

'yan kama pl. ('dan kama m.s.)   fl

Considered by many the funniest of the Hausa comedians (cf. na uwale, masu tandu, 'yan gambara and
'yan galura). They perform individually or in
groups of up to five, catching gifts of money and
kola-nuts in their mouths, and accompanying their
songs and acts on kazagi in many areas and on
gangar 'yan kama in Zaria. They wear funny hats,
carry wooden swords and a calabash dipper used for
cooking which they attach to a string of prayer
beads. Reference to food is a central theme in
their humour, e.g., in comic recitations of
prayers and readings from the Koran, and in the
titles they assign themselves, like "Minister of
the Kitchen" or "Brave Man of Porridge." They do
comic imitations of 'yan tauri, 'yan hoto and popular singers, for example, Shata. When imitating
the dancing and spirit possession of 'yan bori,
they blow through the open end of their drums to
make a sound like goge, which is played for bori.
They perform in daylight in markets, on the
streets and at the homes of sarakuna, attajirai
and harlots. They make extensive annual tours
just after the harvest and later, during the hot
season (cin rani). See 'yankamanci.

Zabiyar <u>Sarki</u> = Zabayar <u>Sarki</u>   cm

A professional singer of praise songs for an Emir
at the <u>waza</u> and <u>buki</u> of his wives, and for all of
the royal cavalcades (<u>hawan salla</u>, <u>hawan daushe</u>,
and <u>hawan kilisa</u>). She sings every day while escorting the Emir from the wives' quarter of the
palace to the Council Chamber and back again.
This was not a title requiring a turbanning (<u>na'din
sarauta</u>) and the post is now vacant in Zaria. At
the court of the Emir of Katsina the post is
filled. See <u>zabiya</u>, <u>marok'an sarakuna</u>, and
<u>marok'an Sarki</u>.

4) <u>Marok'an baki</u> ("acclamators")

<u>bamba'dawa</u> pl. (<u>babam'bade</u> m.s.)   cm/fl
= <u>bamba'de</u> m.s., <u>bamba'do</u> m.s.)

Professional panegyrists who traditionally praise
in the Fulani language (and still do in Zaria), as
opposed to other sorts of <u>marok'an baki</u> who perform in Hausa. Their vocalized acclamations are
performed in a high, rather singsong, falsetto-
like voice, and they do not play musical instruments, though they may combine in performance with
instrumentalists. The performance of their craft
is called <u>bamba'danci</u>. Their patrons are chiefly
Fulani officials; however, they do <u>bamba'danci</u>
from time to time at <u>buki</u> of other settled Fulani
and at the camps of the cattle-herding Fulani.
<u>Bamba'dawa</u> are assigned a higher place in the hi-
erarchy of rank of the royal musicians than the
<u>marok'an baki</u>, due to their association with the
Fulani heritage of much of the senior officialdom.
The head of the royal <u>bamba'dawa</u> of the Emir of
Zaria, the <u>Sarkin Bamba'dawa</u> is not only senior to
the head of the <u>marok'an baki</u>, the <u>San K'ira</u>, but
has the right to appoint his successor. The
<u>Sarkin Bamba'dawa</u> and his assistants perform on
such occasions as Thursday evening <u>waza</u>, turbannings (<u>na'din sarauta</u>) and, ideally, each morning
in front of the palace. For other occasions of
performance see <u>marok'an sarakuna</u> and <u>marok'an
Sarki</u>.

kaskar karen marok'a f.s.   t
("tick of the dog of the marok'a")

An acclamator (marok'in baki) who specializes in
rok'o of karen marok'a. "Tick-like," he sticks
close to the karen marok'a to receive a share of
his earnings.

marok'an baki pl.   fl/cm
(marok'in baki m.s.)
= 'yan k'ira pl. ('dan k'ira m.s.)
= San K'ira m.s.
= masu kirari pl. (mai kirari m.s.)
= 'yan ma'abba pl.
('dan ma'abba or ma'abba m.s.)

Professional acclamators, any marok'a who shout
laudatory epthets (kirari) in the Hausa language
(cf. bamba'dawa) but do not sing or play a musical
instrument, though they often combine in performance with instrumentalists. Some are court panegyrists for officialdom, but most are freelance
performers for the general public, on such occasions as aure, suna, buki, na'din sarauta, tashen
azumi, rawan 'yan mata, wasan misisi, kwanta,
dambe, kokawa, bori, ajo, gayya, kalankuwa, rawan
kashewa, and rawan Gane. See bamba'dawa, San
K'ira, 'yan agalanda, kaskar karen marok'a and
mawak'an bodo.

mawak'an bodo pl.   fl/cm
(mawak'in bodo m.s.)

Marok'an baki in Zaria who do acclamation in a
high singsong voice like bamba'dawa but in the
Hausa language; a comparatively rare style of acclamation which is said to be dying out. Two of
them in Zaria are marok'a of a high official.

San K'ira m.s.   cm/fl

    (i) Any marok'in baki.

    (ii) The title of the chief of the marok'an baki
         for officialdom, e.g., San K'iran Sarkin
         Zazzau ("San K'ira of the Emir of Zaria").

'yan agalanda pl.   fl
('dan agalanda m.s.)

Marok'an baki who call the praises of youth at
boxing (dambe), wrestling matches (kokawa) and
farmwork bees (gayya).

5) 'Yan magana ("talkers")

'yan gambara pl.   fl
('dan gambara m.s., gugurugu m.s.)

Professional satirists who perform mainly in markets, using metric speech for recitations contain-
ing considerable gamtsi and zambo (See gambara,
Section V, 2.542.). They accompany themselves on
gambara (= tallabe) and their bands may also number additional tallabe players, plus one or more
masu kalangu, 'yan kazagi and marok'an baki. They
also perform for the feasts (buki) of wealthy and
generous persons, turbannings (na'din sarauta) of
high officials, and at harlots' houses at night.

'yan garura pl. ('dan garura m.s.)   fl/cm
= 'yan galura pl. ('dan galura m.s.)
= 'yan kacikaura pl.
('dan kacikaura m.s.)
= Malan Na Buta m.s. = na buta m.s.

A large class of professional comedian-acclamators
who speak rapidly and rhythmically or occasionally
sing while accompanying themselves with a hand-
held rattle called buta or galura. Like 'yan
gambara, they praise their sponsors and castigate
their sponsors' enemies in a particularly bawdy
and amusing fashion. Some also dance lewdly while
stripped to the waist. They most often perform in
markets for wealthy traders and merchants and
their clientele and they are reputed for quickly
turning their praise to ridicule (zambo) when
gifts are not forthcoming. Many also perform regularly for officialdom and a few have received
titles from them, e.g., Sarkin Buta and Wazirin
Buta. Prior to January 1966, some also performed
at political party gatherings (wasan N.P.C. or
N.E.P.U.).

<u>Wasa</u> - 'dan <u>gambara</u> to <u>na</u> <u>buta</u>:

<u>Ba</u> <u>buta</u> <u>ba</u> <u>ko</u> <u>randa</u> ne <u>ba</u> <u>yai</u> nama haka <u>ba</u>
"Neither a pot nor a kettle can do this
   to us."

<u>na</u> <u>buta</u> reply:

<u>Ba</u> <u>gambara</u> <u>ba</u> <u>ko</u> <u>dunhun</u> <u>sak'i</u> ne <u>ba</u> <u>kai</u>
<u>mana</u> <u>haka</u> <u>ba</u>
"Neither a fancy cloth nor a plain one can
   do this to us."

<u>'yan</u> <u>kacikaura</u> pl.   fl
(<u>'dan</u> <u>kacikaura</u> m.s.)

A synonym for <u>'yan</u> <u>garura</u> or <u>na</u> <u>buta</u> in Zaria. In
Katsina, where the term is commonly used, they ac-
company themselves with a different type of rattle
called <u>kacikaura</u>.

<u>'yan</u> <u>magana</u>   fl

<u>Marok'i</u> who talk rapidly and rhythmically, prais-
ing or ridiculing persons. Occasionally accompany
talk with rattle like <u>na</u> <u>buta</u>.

C. OFFICES AND TITLES OF PERFORMERS

Introduction

Court musicians and acclamators, in particular, are
often addressed or referred to by title of office. Office
or position (<u>sarauta</u>) is signified by a title and a ceremonial turbanning (<u>na'din</u> <u>sarauta</u>) at the hands of the
dispensing authority. Certain titles are used repeatedly
from top to bottom of Hausa society. Though musicians and
acclamators enjoy comparatively low rank, those who are
clients of officialdom often hold titles similar to their
high-ranking patrons, e.g., <u>Sarki</u>, <u>Waziri</u>, <u>Galadima</u>,
<u>Magaji</u>, <u>Ciroma</u>, <u>'Dan</u> <u>Galadima</u>, <u>Sarkin</u> <u>Fada</u>, <u>Turaki</u>, etc.,

though, of course, they may be differentiated by additional terms, as in Sarkin Maka'da or Wazirin Banga. The full title of a performer would include the title of his patron, e.g., the head of the masu banga, the Magajin Banga, of the Galadima of Zazzau (Zaria) would have the full title of Magajin Bangan Galadiman Zazzau. These complete titles are rarely used and are not included here.

Though titles are much more common among court musicians of officialdom than among musicians of the general public, not all court musicians (particularly assistant) have titles. These are usually named by the addition of the prefixes mai (sing.) and masu (pl.) to the name of their instruments, e.g., mai banga or masu banga. Some non-court musicians have been turbanned by officialdom and hold titles, e.g., Sarkin Maka'da, and they are usually found among drummers of farmers (masu gangar noma) and drummers of butchers (masu kalangu). In addition, some heads among court musicians have "acting" titles, i.e., they have not yet been turbanned, usually because they have not accumulated enough wealth to do so. Among other kinds of musicians, one occasionally encounters a musician who has a self-appointed office and title, though the public is aware that they have not been properly installed in office.

Some court musicians move with their patron when he is promoted to a new sarauta, but most prefer to continue to reside in the same place under their patron's successor. The titles of officialdom and musicians of Zaria are those current in 1963-64; the titles of the official musicians of the court of the Emir of Katsina are those current in 1965.

Bikon Tambari

> Head of tambari drummers of the Emir of Abuja, a non-professional. See Sarkin Tambari, Tambura, Magajin Tambari.

Magajin Banga

> 1. Head of masu banga of the Emirs of Katsina and Zaria. The principal assistant of these heads has the sarauta title of Madakin Banga.

> 2. Head of masu banga of the Galadima, a high senior official resident in Zaria City.

3. Head of masu banga of the District Heads of
   Ikara, Zangon Katab, Soba, Lere, Sabon Gari,
   Kubau, and Zaria City. The head of masu banga of
   the District Head of Kauru atypically has the title of Galadiman Banga. Sarauta titles of assistant masu banga of several District Heads:
   Madakin Banga; Wazirin Banga; Galadiman Banga;
   and Ciroman Banga.

See marok'an Sarki, marok'an sarakuna.

Magajin Busa

1. Head of masu farai of the Emir of Zaria.

2. Senior masu algaita of several District Heads in
   Zaria; however, the head of the performing ensemble -- composed of masu gangar algaita as well as
   masu algaita -- often holds the sarauta title of
   Sarkin Maka'da. Lesser sarauta titles held by
   masu algaita are Madakin Busa, Turakin Busa and
   Ma'ajin Busa.

Magajin Kotso

Head of masu kotso of the District Heads of Kubau
and Igabi in Zaria. The sarauta title of a principal assistant of the Magajin Kotso at Kubau is
Wazirin Kotso. See Sarkin Maka'dan Kotso.

San K'ira

1. Chief of the marok'an baki for officialdom.

2. The head of the royal marok'an baki of the Emir
   of Zaria, San K'iran Zazzau, whose assistants
   hold the following lesser titles: Wazirin Rok'o;
   Madakin Rok'o; Galadiman Rok'o; Sarkin Fadan San
   K'iran Zazzau; and Wakilin Rok'o.

See marok'an Sarki.

Sarkin Bamba'dawa

Head of bamba'dawa in Katsina and Zaria. The assistants of the Sarkin Bamba'dawa of the Emir of
Zaria hold the following lesser sarauta titles:

Dunkan Bamba'dawa; 'Dan Galadiman Bamba'dawa; and
Ciroman Bamba'dawa. See marok'an Sarki.

Sarkin Busa

1. Head of masu k'aho of the Emir of Zaria, who is
   also chief of all royal marok'a (marok'an Sarki)
   and, by extension, all marok'a in the emirate.

2. Head of royal masu kakaki in Katsina. His principal assistant previously held the sarauta title
   of 'Dan Home.

Sarkin Buta

Head of na buta (= 'yan garura) of the District Head
of Sabon Gari of Zaria City. The sarauta title of
his principal assistant is Wazirin Buta. See
marok'an sarakuna.

Sarkin Farai

Head of masu farai in Katsina.

Sarkin Gardi

Head of the Emir of Zaria's snake-charmers; who is
reckoned as one of masartan Sarki. His principal
assistant has the sarauta title of Madakin Gardi.

Sarkin Goge

Heads of masu goge in Zaria City.

1. One such sarauta title-holder, Sarkin Gogen Tudun
   Wada, was turbanned by his principal patron, the
   Chief of the Strangers' Quarter (Sarkin Tudun
   Wada).

2. Two others with the title, Sarkin Gogen N.P.C.,
   were clients and regular performers for the local
   political party organizations of the Northern
   People's Congress.

Sarkin Jauje

1. Head of masu jauje of the Emir of Zaria. His principal assistant has the sarauta title of Madakin Jauje.

2. Head of masu jauje of the District Heads of Ikara, Kacia and Kauru. Lesser sarauta titles of assistants of the head at Kacia are Madakin Jauje and Ciroman Jauje.

See marok'an Sarki, marok'an sarakuna.

Sarkin Kakaki

Head of masu kakaki of the following officials in Zaria:

1. Sarkin Zazzau, the Emir of Zaria. The principal assistant of the Emir's Sarkin Kakaki has the sarauta title of Madakin Kakaki.

2. Galadiman Zazzau, a very high official under the Emir.

3. Sarkin Kauru (District Head of a former vassal kingdom).

See Sarkin Busa, marok'an Sarki.

Sarkin Kalangu

Head of masu kalangun Sarki of the Emir of Zaria. In 1964 this position was filled by an acting head who had not been turbanned. See marok'an Sarki.

Sarkin Ki'dan Caji

Sarauta title of a Caji singer turbanned by his patron, the District Head of Sabon Gari in Zaria. Normally such freelance singers are not turbanned. See mawak'an Caji, yaron Caji and marok'an sarakuna.

Sarkin Maka'da

1. Head of royal marok'a in Katsina.

2. Head of masu gangar fada of the Emirs of Zaria
and Katsina. The sarauta title of their principal assistant is Madakin Ki'da in Zaria and
Wazirin Ki'da in Katsina.

3. Head of masu gangar fada of District Heads of
former vassal states (Kajuru and Kauru) in Zaria.
Lesser sarauta titles of assistants of the Head
at Kajuru: Madakin Ki'da; Turakin Ki'da; 'Dan
Galadiman Ki'da.

4. Head and usually lead singer of a band composed
of masu algaita and masu gangar algaita of Zaria
District Heads of Ikara, Zangon Katab, Giwa,
Makarfi, Lere, Zaria City and environs. Lesser
sarauta titles of assistant masu gangan algaita
of Heads at Lere and Giwa: Madak'in Ki'da;
Makaman Ki'da and Wazirin Ganga. The latter ti-
tle is also held by a mai gangar algaita of the
District Head of Kagarko where there is no Sarkin
Maka'da.

5. Head of masu kalangu of the Chief of the Strangers' Quarter (Tudun Wada) of Zaria. Though he
is most often called Sarkin Maka'da, his full title is Sarkin Maka'dan Tudun Wada.

6. Head of all of the masu kalangu of Zaria, who was
turbanned by the Chief of the Butchers (Sarkin
Pawan Zazzau). His full title is Sarkin Maka'dan
Sarkin Pawan Zazzau.

7. Number 5 and 6 above are occasionally addressed
as Sarkin Kalangu.

See marok'an sarakuna, marok'an Sarki, Sarkin
Kalangu.

Sarkin Maka'dan Gangar Noma

Sarauta title of several heads of masu gangar noma
turbanned by District Heads within the Emirate of
Zaria. One such head, Garba, the Sarkin Maka'dan
Gangar Noma of Mak'arfi District, is a well-known
singer. See Sarkin Maka'dan Gangar Noman Zazzau.

Sarkin Maka'dan Gangar Noman Zazzau

Head of all of the masu gangar noma of Zaria and
turbanned by the Emir. However, he is not consid-

ered one of the regular marok'an Sarki, though he
performs for the Emir on such occasions as royal
cavalcades (hawan daushe and hawan salla).

Sarkin Maka'dan Kotso

Head of masu kotso of the Emir of Katsina. See
Magajin Kotso, marok'an Sarki.

Sarkin Tambari

1. Head of tambari drummers of the Emir of Zaria, a
   non-professional.

2. Head of tambari drummers of the Chief of the former vassal kingdom of Kajuru, now a district of
   Zaria. He is also a non-professional.

See tambari, Bikon Tambari, Tambura, marok'an Sarki.

Sarkin Taushi = Sarkin Tabshi

1. Head of the masu taushi of the Emirs of Katsina
   and Zaria. The principal assistant of the Sarkin
   Taushi of the Emir of Zaria holds the sarauta title of Madakin Taushi.

2. Head of masu taushi of the District Head of Kubau
   in Zaria. Lesser sarauta titles of his assistants are Madakin Taushi and Ciroman Taushi.

See marok'an Sarki, marok'an sarakuna.

Tambura

Head of tambari drummers of the Emir of Katsina, a
non-professional musician.

III. Patrons

Example: Farmers

manoma pl. (manomi m.s.)

1. (Description)

   Farmers.

2. (Musicians traditionally patronized)

   masu gangar noma.

3. (Occasions)

   gayya, kalankuwa.

4. (Role of patron and miscellaneous)

   Either as an individual or as a
   member of a class they may act as
   a sponsor of take.

attajirai pl. (attajiri m.s.)

1. Wealthy merchants.

2. As individuals, attajirai patronize all sorts of
   marok'a and, along with sarakuna, they are the principal patrons of famous singers, who often compose
   special songs for them.

3. buki, tashen azumi, yawon salla. May be visited any
   time by touring musicians.

karuwai pl. (karuwa f.s.)

1. Harlots.

2. All sorts of marok'a, especially masu kukuma and masu goge.

3. Any time and on special occasions, such as yawon salla and tashen azumi.

4. One or more men may act as sponsor of kirari for a favorite karuwa, and competition among sponsors may develop. Karuwai also may act as sponsors of kirari (for themselves).

   Harlots sometimes play the kukuma or shantu for themselves and their patrons.

maharba pl. (maharbi m.s.)
= 'yan farauta pl. ('dan farauta m.s.)

1. Hunters.

2. masu komo.

3. buki, bago, na'din sarauta, hawan salla.

4. Either as an individual or as a member of a class they may act as a sponsor of take, termed taken maharba, and engage in self-praise (kirari).

mahauta pl. (mahauci m.s.)
= 'yan fawa pl. ('dan fawa m.s.)
= rundawa pl. (barunje m.s.)

1. Butchers.

2.a. masu kalangu.

   b. see also maka'dan 'yan tauri.

3. ki'dan fawa (= ki'dan nama), buki, hawan k'aho, na'din sarauta, tashen azumi. (Since 'yan dambe are most often butchers, dambe /boxing/ may also be included here.)

4. Either as an individual or as a member of a class, they may act as a sponsor of take, called taken mahauta.

mak'era pl. (mak'eri m.s.)

1. Blacksmiths.

2. 'yan dundufa.

3. buki, na'din sarauta, aure, suna, tashen azumi,
dry season tours (cin rani); visits the chief of
the blacksmiths (Sarkin Mak'era) each Friday after
the mosque (gaisuwar juma'a).

4. May act as sponsors of kirari and take, called taken
mak'era.

malamai pl. (malami m.s.)

1. Islamic teachers and scholars specializing in either
Koranic studies or other branches of learning.

2. masu ki'dan buta.

3. watan azumi, K'aramar Salla, Babbar Salla.

4. As member of a class they may act as sponsor of
ki'dan malamai.

manoma pl. (manomi m.s.)

1. Farmers.

2. masu gangar noma.

3. gayya, kalankuwa, buki.

4. Either as an individual or as a member of a class,
they may act as a sponsor of take and engage in
self-praise (kirari).

marok'a pl.
(marok'i m.s., marokiya f.s.)

1. Professional instrumentalists and vocalists. See
marok'a, II-A.

2. karen marok'a.

3. aure, buki, suna, tashen azumi, yawon salla.

4. May act as sponsor of kirari.

masu wasa da kura pl.
(mai wasa da kura m.s.)
= gardawan kura pl.
(gardin kura m.s.)

1. Conjurer who wrestles with, and ostensibly tames, hyenas in the market place.

2. maka'dan mai wasa da kura = maka'dan gardin kura.

3. wasan kura in the market place (kasuwa).

Northern Peoples Congress (N.P.C.) and
Northern Elements Progressive Union (N.E.P.U.)

1. Major political parties in northern Nigeria prior to the first military coup of January 1966.

2. masu goge and masu kukuma with 'yan k'warya and na buta.

3. All party functions, especially rawan kashewa, wasan N.P.C. or wasan N.E.P.U. and visits of important politicians for political rallies and the like.

   Note: all kinds of marok'a performed at large political rallies, including a party poet, mawak'an N.P.C., and famous singer/instrumentalists like Ibrahim Na Habu, who bore the title, probably self-bestowed, of Sarkin Wak'ar N.P.C. ("The Chief Singer for the N.P.C.").

samari pl. (saurayi m.s.)

1. Young men.

2. masu kwairama, masu kalangu, masu gangar noma and masu tallabe.

3. rawan 'yan mata, buki, rawan misisi, kalankuwa, rawan Gane, a sha k'afa, kokawa, dambe, ajo and gayya.

4. As individuals, they often act as a sponsor of their own take (taken samari).

sarakuna pl. (basarake m.s.)
= saraki pl. = sarakai pl.
= masarauta pl.

1. Any officeholder whose installation is marked by the
   receipt of a title and a ceremonial turbanning at
   the hands of his patron or the deputy of the latter.
   Such patrons of marok'a are normally Emirs and high
   officials under them, resident in the capital, and
   district heads, resident in district capitals. Village heads of Zaria and Katsina ordinarily do not
   have their own musicians, but village heads in certain villages of historical importance do (e.g.,
   Kurfi, Gazobi, Lere, etc.).

2. marok'an sarakuna, marok'an Sarki, marok'an hakimai,
   marok'an fada.

3. waza (= sara), wazan salla, yawo, yawon salla, hawan
   salla, hawan daushe, hawan kilisa, buki, na'din
   sarauta, suna, aure. Annual inspection tours
   (rangadi) and official business trips of the Emir
   and District Heads.

4. Officeholders act as sponsors of special take (taken
   sarakuna) associated with their sarauta title. They
   also act as sponsors of kirari and of songs composed
   not only by their own musicians but also by famous
   freelance singers.

'yan bori pl.
('dan bori m.s., 'yar bori f.s.)

1. Male and female initiates of the bori spirit possession cult.

2. masu garayan bori, masu goge, masu duman girke, 'yan
   k'warya, masu kasam'bara, masu gora.

3. rawan bori, hawan bori and girka.

4. Initiates and spectators sponsor kirari for themselves and for spirits (iskoki).

'yan dambe pl. ('dan dambe m.s.)

1. Boxers; most are local amateurs, but some are famous
   and travel widely, e.g., Shago, now retired, and his
   well-known singer, 'Dan Anace.

2. masu kalangu.

3. dambe.

4. They act as sponsors of take or kirari performed at boxing events, or when the boxer is a spectator of the girls' dancing (rawan 'yan mata). They also praise themselves (kirari) when excited by praise of marok'a.

'yan hoto pl. ('dan hoto m.s.)

1. Strong men, conjurers and dancers who perform in farming costume and usually perform tricks with a hand-plough. Since they are primarily farmers they normally perform and tour (cin rani) after the harvest.

2. masu gangar noma with masu kazagi and with marok'an baki.

3. wasan 'yan hoto, kalankuwa, K'aramar Salla and any large public gathering.

4. They act as sponsors of take or kirari and praise themselves when excited by praise of marok'a.

'yan mata pl. ('yar mata f.s.)

1. Unmarried young women and girls.

2. maka'dan 'yan mata, masu kalangu, masu kwairama, and masu gangar noma (rare today).

3. rawan 'yan mata, wasan misisi, kalankuwa, kwanta (= kwance), kai gara and buki.

4. 'yan mata may dance and/or perform wak'ar 'yan mata. Some 'yan mata have their personal take sponsored by themselves, by older female kin or by a suitor.

'yan kokawa pl. ('dan kokawa m.s.)
= 'yan kokuwa pl. ('dan kokuwa m.s.)

1. Wrestlers.

2. masu kwairama.

3. <u>kokawa</u>.

4. They act as sponsors of <u>take</u> and <u>kirari</u> and praise
themselves when stimulated with praise by <u>marok'a</u>.

<u>'yan</u> <u>tauri</u> pl. ('<u>dan</u> <u>tauri</u> m.s.)
= <u>k'ufegeru</u> pl. (<u>k'ufegere</u> m.s.)

1. Famous for their powerful medicine, which is said to
make them invulnerable to attack by any sort of me-
tallic or other hard object. They exhibit their
powers in public competitions, <u>wasan</u> <u>'yan</u> <u>tauri</u>, and
act as bodyguards to important officials. Most of
them are either butchers or hunters.

2. <u>maka'dan</u> <u>'yan</u> <u>tauri</u>.

3. <u>wasan</u> <u>'yan</u> <u>tauri</u>, <u>buki</u>, <u>na'din</u> <u>sarauta</u>, <u>hawan</u> <u>salla</u>,
<u>daba</u>, <u>ki'dan</u> <u>mahauta</u> and <u>dambe</u>.

4. Either as individuals or as a member of a social
group they may act as sponsor of <u>take</u> and <u>kirari</u>.
They also praise themselves when excited with praise
by <u>marok'a</u>.

IV. Occasions

Explanation of Numerical Indices

Name(s) of occasion (alphabetized headings)

1. Description of social context of performance, venue, and, if necessary, am-
   plification of performer's role beyond
   information given in Section II, Part B.

2. Time of performance.

3. Class of performers.

ajo (d.f. Yoruba)
= jama'iyar neman arziki

1. A public meeting and entertainment organized by a
   bridegroom's friends to raise money to meet marriage
   expenses and held on the streets of larger towns in
   front of the entrance house of his residence, or in
   halls or hotels hired for the purpose. Friends of
   the bridegroom, encouraged by praise of him and his
   family by professional acclamators, singers and
   their bands, subscribe money, the amount being announced to the gathering with words of praise for
   the donor by an acclamator. It is understood that
   the bridegroom will attend future ajo of his friends
   and not only reciprocate but also give a subscrip-
   tion greater than the one he himself received.

2. Held in the evening of the buki or up to several
   days afterwards.

3. All sorts of marok'a, as above, especially popular
   singers and instrumentalists, who can draw a crowd.

<u>a</u> <u>sha</u> <u>k'afa</u> ("to drink the feet")
= <u>kwambe</u>

1. A dance done by young men which is also a kind of
   foot-boxing. They whirl on one foot with the other
   foot outstretched causing the circle of spectators
   to expand (<u>sharan</u> <u>fage</u>). Sometimes they hit their
   opposites with considerable force as in the following <u>kirari</u> for a victor:

   > <u>Ga</u> <u>mai</u> <u>tambari</u> <u>da</u> <u>sawu</u> <u>ga</u> <u>mai</u> <u>duka</u> <u>a</u> <u>fa'di</u>
   > "Here is the <u>tambari</u> drummer who beats with
   > his foot and knocks his opponent to the
   > ground."

2. Any evening, often after the girls finish dancing
   (<u>rawan</u> <u>'yan</u> <u>mata</u>).

3. <u>masu</u> <u>kalangu</u>, <u>'yan</u> <u>kuntuku</u>, <u>masu</u> <u>kwairama</u> and
   <u>marok'an</u> <u>baki</u>.

<u>aure</u>

Hausa marriage. Though the rituals of marriage are
numerous, varied, and complex, some of the basic
ones may be outlined here in more or less chronolog-
ical order:

a. <u>baiwa</u>

   1. Public betrothal, which is usually held in the
      morning in the residence of the girl's parents,
      and carried out by representatives of both the
      boy and the girl and witnessed by Koranic
      scholars and guests. Sometimes the date of
      the marriage (<u>sa</u> <u>rana</u>) is set at this time.
      <u>Marok'a</u> in attendance announce the betrothal
      and then call for prayers.

   2. Often held more than a year before the actual
      marriage.

   3. Different classes of <u>marok'a</u> may attend, espe-
      cially those traditionally tied to the boy and
      his family.

b. <u>sa</u> <u>rana</u>

   1. Literally to "set the date" of the marriage, a
      ritual which is usually held in the morning in
      the residence of the girl's parents. <u>Marok'a</u>

announce the date, shout blessings and call
for prayers.

2. Held either at the same time of the betrothal
(baiwa) or between betrothal and marriage.

3. As for the baiwa.

c. 'daurin aure (= aure)

1. Literally "the tying of the marriage," the actual marriage ceremony, which is usually held
in the morning in the residence of the bride's
parents. Marok'a announce the amount of the
sadaki (a marriage payment), the witnessing of
the marriage and the commencement of prayers.

2. Usually after the harvest of cash crops; the
day of the month is set by a Koranic scholar.

3. Same as for the baiwa.

d. tarewa

1. Bridal procession to the husband's house held
later in the day of 'daurin aure. The girls
accompanying the bride sometimes sing special
songs.

2. As above.

3. Normally no professional musicians are present.

e. buki (= biki)

1. The marriage feast (bukin aure) held in the
evening at the husband's residence (another
buki is held by the bride's parents but it is
not as important from the standpoint of the
performance of music). Marok'a perform outside the entrance hut (zaure), where they drum
for the dancing of the girls and/or provide
music for an ajo. Sometimes a professional
female singer (e.g., masu amada) performs in
the inner residential quarter for the married
women. The latter may perform their own songs,
accompanying themselves with drumming on calabashes (k'warya).

2. As above.

3. Many classes of marok'a may attend, especially those traditionally tied to the bridegroom or his family.

f. kai gara

1. Procession of girls and women transporting the bride's dowry to her husband's residence. A drummer(s) marches in front of the procession with one or more professional acclamators (marok'an baki), and the latter shout the contents of the dowry for the public to hear. The girls sing in leader and chorus response style. The drummer may stay for a while at the husband's house to accompany dancing of the girls (rawan 'yan mata).

2. Held in the morning, usually about one week after the 'daurin aure.

3. masu kalangu and masu k'wairama.

Babbar Salla

1. An annual festival ('Id el Kabir) which, like the companion festival of K'aramar Salla, is an occasion for the performance of music, ranging from music of the court to music for butchers; but ordinarily there is less musical activity than at K'aramar Salla. See tambari for customs related to the performance on royal drums in various emirates.

2. On the 10th day of Zul hajji.

3. Many classes of professional and non-professional musicians.

bago

1. A bush-drive in which a large group of hunters (maharba) surround game or drive them with bushfires. The lutenists of the hunters (masu komo) perform their patron's take around the campfire the night previous and accompany them to the hunting place, playing en route.

2. Harvest time (kaka).

3. masu komo.

bori

1. A spirit possession cult whose male and female members ('yan bori) must undergo an initiation (girka). The initiates, mostly women, are possessed (hawa, lit. "mounted") while dancing by various spirits (iskoki) or gods of the bori pantheon, which is headed by the spirit called Sarkin Maka'da ("The Chief of the Drummers"), in contradistinction to the status hierarchy of real life. Marok'a play an important part in bori rites, providing the drumming for dancing (ki'dan bori) and the praising of iskoki in song (wak'ar bori) and in speech. Many Hausa patronize these ceremonies to cure physical and psychological ailments and also simply for excitement and entertainment. Iskoki are also called to give blessings on the establishment of a market or for a wedding when married women may perform ki'dan ruwa to accompany the dancing.

2. Throughout the year; less during the farming season. Held for a few days during K'aramar Salla and Babbar Salla, and, of course, for girka.

3. masu garaya, masu gora, masu kasam'bara, masu goge, 'yan k'warya and marok'an baki.

buki = biki

1. Any celebratory feast, such as aure or suna, which often involves performance of celebratory music by both marok'a and non-professionals.

2. Aure (marriage) feasts occur usually after the cash crop harvests. Suna (naming) feasts, of course, occur anytime.

3. Different classes of marok'a may attend, especially those traditionally tied to the hosts. Wealthy persons often have popular singers and instrumentalists for these occasions.

cin rani ("eating the dry season")

1. Professional tours during the dry season after the agricultural work is done. All sorts of musicians make extensive tours at this time. They commonly make two annual tours: one just after the food-crop harvests and another after the cash-crop harvests, when the markets are especially active and money

relatively plentiful. <u>Marok'a</u> also use the term <u>yawo</u> for travelling from one patron to another, and court musicians accompany their patrons on bush inspection tours called <u>rangadi</u>.

<u>daba</u> (d.f. Durbar)

1. A cavalcade, like <u>hawan salla</u> below, held in honour of a visiting dignitary.

2. Anytime.

3. <u>Marok'an Sarki</u> and other low-ranking clients of the Emir make up the procession.

<u>da'be</u>

1. Flattening and finishing an earthen floor, work by women to the accompaniment of song (<u>wak'ar da'be</u>).

2. Anytime.

3. Non-professionals.

<u>dambe</u>

1. Boxing by young butchers or hunters. Famous boxers like Shago (now retired) tour with their musicians, some of whom are famous in their own right, like 'Dan Anace, Shago's praise singer. Local boxers have resident <u>marok'a</u> play for them. Before the boxing begins, the drummers play the boxer's <u>take</u>, the acclamators shout their praises, and, sometimes, songs of praise are sung. Seemingly excited by all of this praise, the boxer begins to tremble (<u>tsuma</u>) and, with arms outstretched, shouts his own praises (<u>kirari</u>). The musicians also issue a challenge (<u>kiranye</u>) in behalf of the boxer. The drumming is stopped during the boxing and resumed after it is finished in honour of the victor.

2. After the harvest and, again, in the case of local boxers, during <u>K'aramar Salla</u> and <u>Babbar Salla</u>.

3. <u>masu kalangu</u>, <u>marok'an baki</u> and <u>'yan agalanda</u>.

gaisuwar juma'a

1. A visit by a marok'i or other client to a patron's home to greet him as a token of respect.

2. After the prayers held at the mosque on Friday.

3. Any marok'a, especially those tied to a distinct class of patrons.

gayya = gayyar noma

1. Cooperative farm work by rural youth, e.g., making ridges for planting cotton with large hand-ploughs (garma). Occasionally gayya are concerned with public works, such as clearing paths, and work of this kind may also be done in the city. Though the work is often hard, a festive atmosphere prevails. The host, who is often a Village Head or a District Head, provides refreshments and the girls come out to view the proceedings and to encourage the workers by singing praise songs, though the latter is less common today. Drummers beat the personal take of workers and often sing their words and acclamators shout kirari. A worker (particularly a 'dan hoto) will stop, quiver a moment, and with his arms outstretched, praise himself before working mightily again.

2. The farming season (damina, lit. the "rainy season").

3. masu gangar noma, 'yan kazagi and marok'an baki.

hawan daushe

1. Similar to hawan salla below, but held two days later.

hawan kilisa

1. A cavalcade like hawan salla below, but on a smaller scale and done for "pleasure."

2. Anytime.

3. Marok'an Sarki with some other courtiers.

hawan salla

1. Royal cavalcade from the palace of the Emir of Zaria
   to the praying ground outside the city walls and
   back again, and from the palace of the Emir of
   Katsina to the central mosque and back again, and
   made up of high-ranking officialdom and their clients.

2. Annual Muslim feasts of K'aramar Salla ('Id el Fitr)
   and Babbar Salla ('Id el Kabir).

3. Marok'an sarakuna -- many of whom are on horseback
   -- plus some other classes of musicians: masu komo,
   maka'dan 'yan tauri, masu goge, mawak'an Caji and
   zabiyoyi.

kalankuwa

1. A harvest-time festival of the rural youth which
   varies in scope and content. In Zaria, it seems to
   have been associated with actual co-operative farm
   work (gayya), but today all one normally encounters
   is mock farm labour by village youths in which
   tricks and feats of strength with hand ploughs are
   done in late afternoon in a field next to the village or in the village square itself. The performers are encouraged by the drumming of their take and
   the shouting of their kirari. Touring 'yan hoto,
   who perform the most elaborate feats of strength as
   well as sundry acts of magic (wasan 'yan hoto), are
   sometimes the only performers. This may be followed by wrestling (kokawa) or boxing (dambe) and in
   the evening a kwanta and wasan misisi, and gambling
   and goge music may be added to the evening's entertainment.

2. As above.

3. Masu gangar noma, 'yan kazagi, and marok'an baki for
   the farming play and 'yan hoto performance. See the
   other occasions for other classes of performers.

K'aramar Salla

1. An important feast ('Id el Fitr) which marks the
   close of the fast month. Some idea of the variety
   of music performed during this festival may be had
   from the following list of performance occasions re-
   corded for this period in Zaria City in 1964:

hawan salla, hawan daushe, wazan salla, yawon salla, wasan misisi, kwanta, rawan 'yan mata, wasan 'yan hoto, dambe, kokawa, and rawan kashewa. Prior to the festival there is ki'dan fawa in the market and, sometimes, hawan k'aho. For customs related to beating of the royal drums, see tambari.

2. The first day of Shawal; however, many of the above performances take place on succeeding days.

3. Nearly all classes of performers, professional and non-professional.

ki'dan fawa = ki'dan nama

1. Drumming for butchers in the market to attract business or to announce slaughtering. The latter is more often done in smaller communities where slaughtering is not an everyday occurrence. When performing in the market, the drum rhythm (take) may be "saying":

> Ku sai nama
> ku zo da ku'di
> ku sai naman shanu

> "Buy meat
> come with money
> buy meat of the cow."

2. As above. Before important religious feasts (K'aramar Salla, Babbar Salla and Sallar Cika Ciki), they perform in the market and perhaps do ki'dan hawan k'aho for wasan hawan k'aho. In Zaria City, they most often drum in the market on Friday morning and sometimes on Wednesday and Sunday mornings.

3. masu kalangu.

kokawa = kokuwa

1. Wrestling by young men. There is drumming of their take, acclamation (kirari) by marok'an baki and, sometimes, singing of praise songs by the principal drummer (mai kwairama), with the chorus sung by the 'yan kazagi. This normally causes the wrestlers to quiver (tsuma) and to praise themselves before beginning to wrestle.

2. Anytime during the dry season, especially for buki and kalankuwa or when the community head calls for it.

3. As above.

kwanta (kwance)

1. A formal expression of courtship or institutional-ized love-making (tsarance) which is organized by the drummers of the youth at least once a year. In kwanta, which means "untied," the girls sit ("tied") on a mat in front of the drummers in the dancing place (filin rawa) until their boy friends -- or, less impressively, their kinsmen -- "untie" them by giving a gift in their name to the marok'a. A marok'in baki then shouts "he" to stop the drumming and announces, for example, "Abdu has given two shillings to untie Binta."

2. At K'aramar Salla or Babbar Salla or in connection with a harvest-time festival (kalankuwa).

3. masu kalangu, 'yan kuntuku and marok'an baki.

lugude = samammance

1. Rhythmic pounding of any foodstuff by groups of wom-en using one or more mortars (turmi) and each using a pestle. Extra percussive effects are produced by the pestle being struck against the side of the mor-tar on the up-stroke, followed by releasing the hands from the pestle, clapping them, and then catching the pestle for the down-stroke. Elaborated pounding of this kind, with hand-clapping, is con-sidered "drumming," even without song. However, they often sing when doing lugude. Sometimes when a woman is grinding corn (nik'a) while others are do-ing lugude, she will stop, pick up sticks and beat her grinding stone in concert with the others.

2. Done anytime, but usually when preparing food for a naming or marriage feast (buki).

3. Non-professionals.

Mauludu = Maulidi

1. The Prophet's birthday and occasion for performance on tambura in Daura City.

na'din sarauta

1. A ceremonial turbanning at the hands of a dispensing authority upon the occasion of the installation of a person in office and his receipt of a title.

2. No special time of year, but the fast month is a- voided.

3. Marok'a, particularly marok'an sarakuna, are common- ly in attendance at such ceremonies.

nik'a

1. Corn-grinding by women on a stone block (resembling the Middle-American metate). Women often sing to the rhythm of the grinding. Any kind of song can be sung at this time and the words are often improvis- ed. There are flattering or critical songs about a husband or a mother-in-law, and unflattering songs about co-wives (see wak'ar mata).

   A proverb (karin magana) in which nik'a is referred to:

   > Wak'a 'daya ba shi k'are nik'a
   > "One song is not enough to finish the grinding of corn."

2. Year-around.

3. Non-professionals.

rangadi

   See cin rani.

rawan Gane = rawan takai

1. A dance performed by young men and boys throughout Hausaland, accompanied by the beating together of sticks or short iron rods by pairs of dancers to- gether with drumming. In Zaria, the dancers of

rawan Gane wear short grass skirts and ankle rattles
(cakansami) and sing songs abusing wrong-doers
(wak'ar abayyana) in a manner that would not be tol-
erated at any other time.

2. At the end of the rains, or in Zaria during the
month of Gane, the third month in the Muslim calen-
dar.

3. masu gangar noma, masu kwairama and 'yan kazagi.

rawan kashewa = rawan banjo

1. A dance by a group of young men and women hired for
this purpose by a political party and said to have
originated in the city of Jos. Most of the large
cities in Hausaland had such dance teams, which
travelled and competed with one another, performing
often in outdoor courtyards of hotels. Admission
was charged to view these competitions, which were
called rawan kashewa or rawan banjo; however, the
same dance was done in combination with other forms
of entertainment at pre-election campaign meetings
(wasan N.P.C. or N.E.P.U.). A dance team consisted
of separate lines of female and male youths who
danced a series of intricate steps in unison and
each line of dancers was identically costumed in
Western dress. Occasionally the male and female
dancers paired off to dance the twist (tuwis) in the
Western manner.

2. On weekends and, more often, preceding elections.

3. The most usual accompaniment for a performance was
supplied by masu goge, and masu k'waryar goge or by
masu kalangu playing with 'dan kar'bi and 'yan
kuntuku or by an ensemble of both groups of instrumentalists.

rawan 'yan mata

1. Dancing of girls to a number of dance rhythms
(ki'dan 'yan mata) on Friday nights, on any night
during a festival period (K'aramar Salla and Babbar
Salla) and on any pleasant moonlight night. Young
men normally act as spectators at the dancing place
(filin rawa = fagen rawa) and let their interest in
a girl be known by paying the marok'a to call her
out to dance. The girls also dance in connection

with the following occasions: <u>buki</u>, <u>kwanta</u>, <u>kalankuwa</u>, <u>wasan misisi</u> and <u>kai gara</u>.

2. As above.

3. <u>masu kalangu</u>, <u>'yan kuntuku</u>, <u>maka'dan 'yan mata</u> and <u>masu kwairama</u>.

<u>Sallar Cika Ciki</u> = <u>Sallar Wowwo</u>

1. The feast of the new year. <u>Cika ciki</u> means "full belly," the custom being to eat as much as one can at the feast. The drummers of the butchers (<u>masu kalangu</u>) are particularly busy playing for a parade of cattle to be slaughtered, which is usually associated with <u>wasan hawan k'aho</u>. Of course, they also perform for their patrons in the market place (<u>ki'dan fawa</u>).

2. Ninth and 10th of Muharram.

3. As above.

<u>Sallar Takutufa</u> = <u>Sallar Takutaha</u>

1. Prophet's naming day and occasion for performance on <u>tambura</u> in Daura City.

<u>suna</u>

1. A naming ceremony often held in the residence of the father's parents, in the case of a first-born child, or in the father's residence, in the case of subsequent children. Various kinds of music may be performed by <u>marok'a</u> but it is less often done in Zaria since the passage of the Beggar-Minstrel ordinance. Whether or not music is performed, <u>marok'a</u> are called upon to do the following: a) call the assembled for prayer; b) shout blessings for the mother and child to which the assembled respond "<u>amin</u>"; and c) announce the name of the child. In the evening a feast is held which normally involves the performance of music by both <u>marok'a</u> and others (e.g., women and girls).

2. Seven days after childbirth.

3. <u>Marok'a</u> of all kinds, especially those traditionally "tied" to the family, if any.

tashen Azumi = tashe

1. Singing, dancing, blowing and drumming in the streets and in front of homes during the month of Ramadan.

2. Most performances are after the evening meal up to around midnight; however, some stay up later to wake the citizenry so they may prepare food and eat before dawn.

3. Marok'a and non-professional youths, boys and girls, and old men who sing early in the morning.

wasan hawan k'aho = hawan k'aho

1. Entertainment involving acrobatics on and around a large, fierce bull. Prior to important feast days like Sallar Cika Ciki, bulls are paraded through the streets, and young butchers play with them (lit. "ride the horns") in front of generous patrons' homes to the accompaniment of a special kalangu rhythm (ki'dan hawan k'aho) and the shouting of kirari by acclamators. Aside from the entertainment, the purpose of the play is to advertise slaughtering for the feast day. First, the bull is teased to arouse him and to frighten the spectators, and then the drumming becomes faster and the young man leaps over the horns and grabs the bull around the neck. When the play is over, the patron's gift is announced by a marok'in baki and shared between the young performer and the marok'a.

2. As above.

3. masu kalangu, marok'an baki.

wasan kura

1. The wrestling and ostensible taming of hyenas by professional entertainers who perform in markets to the accompaniment of drumming.

2. Any market day.

3. See maka'dan mai wasa da kura.

wasan misisi

1. A "play of the miss or misses" presented by the
youth associations of many wards in Zaria City and
some rural communities, in which the girls dress in
European clothes, nurses' uniforms and the like, and
boys wear all sorts of uniforms of officialdom, of
police, soldiers, doctors, etc. These "titled" persons rule the "commoners" with much horseplay of
mock arrests, trials, fines and other "punishments."
The girls serve tea and biscuits to their boyfriends,
and the singers, drummers and acclamators praise all
of the "titled" persons, the girls singing the chorus responses. The kwanta is then held, followed by
dancing of the girls (rawan 'yan mata). Sometimes,
after the food is consumed, a beauty contest is held
and the winner is given the title of Sarauniyar kyau
and wears a special sash.

2. In the dry season and during K'aramar Salla.

3. mawak'an 'yan mata, masu kalangu, 'yan kuntuku.

wasan N.P.C. or N.E.P.U.

1. A wasa (lit. "play") of the leading political parties (prior to their abolition in January 1966)
which was held to boost membership and/or to raise
money by charging admission. Such occasions vari-
ously included performances by popular singers and
instrumentalists, party poets, comedians, professional dancers (rawan kashewa) and bori drummers and
dancers. Singers and acclamators praised party
leaders, local officials and party supporters and
censured their enemies. There was little speech-
making.

2. Anytime, particularly in the months just preceding
an election.

3. As above.

wasan 'yan hoto

1. Entertainment by 'yan hoto, who are professional
strong men, conjurers and dancers. They perform
stripped to the waist, dressed in leather aprons and
wearing many amulets including an animal horn with
which, it is said, they shoot magic needles. They
perform at kalankuwa, weddings (aure), market places

and join in the work at co-operative-group farming gatherings (gayya). They also come to the city during feast days (K'aramar Salla and Babbar Salla) and some tour widely.

In praise songs they are called masu nakiya da garma ("the throwers and catchers of hand ploughs"), a reference to one of their best-known acts. They also make deep cuts in the soil with hand ploughs and do other feats of strength, such as balancing a heavy log on their heads or carrying, pyramid fashion, two drummers plus their large farm drums on their shoulders. Among their most sensational conjuring acts is one in which a 'dan hoto imbeds a spear upright in the ground and sits and revolves upon the point. Acclamators (marok'an baki) call their kirari and masu gangar noma drummers beat their take and sing praise songs with the 'yan kazagi drummers singing the chorus responses. Perhaps, inspired by all of this commendation, the 'dan hoto begins quivering and, with arms outstretched, praises himself.

2. As above.

3. As above.

wasan 'yan tauri

1. Public exhibitions and competitions of 'yan tauri, in which they display their invulnerability to all sorts of cutlery. It is generally believed that they accomplish this by drinking a secret herbal potion. To demonstrate the effectiveness of their medicine, they attempt to stab themselves with knives and swords, and some are said to even make a blade melt before it pierces the skin. They break razor blades with their fingers or attempt to cut their eyes with razors. They may perform in public places, in front of the homes of generous persons, or at the home of a fellow 'dan tauri upon the occasion of a buki.

2. Anytime, but especially during the dry season.

3. maka'dan 'yan tauri and sometimes masu kalangu.

<u>Watan Azumi</u>
= <u>Watan Azumin Duk Gari</u>

1. <u>Ramadan</u>, the month of fast. Professional, semi-professional and non-professional musicians are active in connection with <u>tashen azumi</u>. Non-professional youths perform more during this month than at any other time of the year.

2. As above.

3. As above.

<u>Watan Azumin Tsoffi</u>

1. Month of <u>Rajab</u> (7th month), beginning and end of which are occasions for the beating of <u>tambura</u> in Daura City.

<u>Watan Takutufa</u> = <u>Watan Takutaha</u>

1. Month of <u>Rabi'i Lawwal</u>, beginning of which is occasion for performance on <u>tambura</u> in Daura City.

<u>Watan Wowwo</u>

1. Month of <u>Muharram</u>, beginning of which is occasion for performance on <u>tambura</u> in Daura City as well as on day of <u>Wowwo</u>.

<u>waza</u> = <u>sara</u>
= <u>ki'dan daren juma'a</u>

1. A weekly, obligatory performance by musicians of officialdom outside their patrons' palace or residence.

2. Usually on Thursday evening (<u>daren juma'a</u>); however, certain classes of royal musicians of the Emir of Zaria perform on other nights of the week (e.g., <u>masu jauje</u>, <u>masu banga</u> and <u>masu taushi</u>).

3. <u>marok'an Sarki</u> and <u>marok'an sarakuna</u>.

wazan salla = saran salla

1. Like a weekly waza, but held on the eve of either K'aramar Salla or Babbar Salla.

yawon salla

1. Lit. the "salla stroll," in which court musicians (marok'an sarakuna) greet their patrons and other senior officials at their residence in expectation of receiving a gift (barka da salla or goron salla). During K'aramar Salla, head court musicians traditionally receive a gown and a turban. Other classes of musicians do yawon salla, too.

2. K'aramar Salla and Babbar Salla, especially the former.

3. Any kind of marok'a, but especially marok'an sarakuna.

V. Music
Performance

For convenience of presentation terms have been
grouped alphabetically within the following categories:

1. General performance features.

2. Vocal music, further subdivided into:

2.1. gangami: proclamation.

2.2. gu'da: ululation.

2.3. kiranye: challenges.

2.4. kirari: acclamation.

2.5. wak'a: song.

3. Instrumental music, further subdivided into:

3.1. bushe-bushe da ki'de-ki'de: blowing and drumming, playing a stringed instrument, and striking or shaking an idiophone.

3.2. miscellanea.

4. Dance.

1. General Performance Features

amo m.s.

The highly resonant quality of the sound-signals of certain instruments, including ganga, kalangu, kotso, tambari, algaita, farai, and kakaki. The main criterion would appear to be the carrying quality of the sound-signals of such instruments. Thus it may be said, for instance, kalangu na amo ("kalangu is reverberating") or kalangu na tashi ("kalangu is rising").

amshi m.s. = amsa f.s.

A chorus response to a solo statement in either vocal or instrumental music, the response in almost all cases being in the nature of a refrain. Thus, in song, a mawak'i ("solo singer") is answered by the masu amshi = 'yan amshi = masu amsawa (the "chorus"), the latter group either merely supplying the refrain as a stanza marker (as in most songs by Alhaji Shata), or else extending and completing the solo section before stating the refrain (as, for instance, in most songs by Sarkin Tabshin Katsina Alhaji Mamman). This is counterparted in instrumental music, e.g., kakaki, where a solo trumpet is sometimes answered by a chorus group of trumpets uniformly pitched at an interval approaching 100 cents higher than the solo instrument.

azanci m.s.

Creative inventiveness in any performance, vocal or instrumental. In vocal music the term is usually applied to a singer's use of language, the terms fasaha and hazik'anci being near-similes.

rok'o m.s. = garam m.s. = zuga f.s.

The professional acclamation of a patron in hope of reward, from which is derived the derogatory term for any professional musician -- marok'i m.s., marok'iya f.s. Such acclamation may take the form of either vocal (kirari, wak'ar yabo) or instrumental (take) music, and in the case of the former is usually compounded of extravagant praise of the patrons'

identity, ancestry, characteristics and prospects.
By a popular extension of meaning the term may be
loosely, and inaccurately, applied to performance by
any professional musician, whether such a performance
is based on praise of a patron or not (cf. wak'ar
nasha'di), and to presentation of himself before his
patron in expectation of reward by a musician without
actual performance. The latter is also termed
raraka, whether done by a musician or non-musician.
The socially acceptable acclamation of God or a human
patron by a cripple or Koranic student is termed
bara.

salo m.s.

The stylistic identity of a composition, compounded
from such features as text (if present), melody,
rhythm, and timbre.

shiri m.s.

The preparation of a composition for performance,
whether vocal or instrumental, including the utter-
ance of a dedicatory prayer (addu'a). In vocal music
shiri may take the form of gunguni; in instrumental
music, jinjina.

2. Vocal Music

2.1. gangami m.s.

An official proclamation ordered by an authority
such as an Emir or a District Head, and announced
by word of mouth with drum accompaniment, usually
on gangar fada. Proclamation by word of mouth a-
lone is known as yekuwa, and is not included herein
since it does not depend on performance by a musician.

a. karin magana:

Tun da ka ji gangami ka tabbata akwai magana
a baya
"Because you have heard the proclamation drummed,

you may be certain there are words behind it,"
i.e., "There's no smoke without fire."

2.2. gu'da m.s.

Celebratory ululating by women, any woman specializing in this being termed magu'diya.

   a. kirarin ango ("kirari for a bridegroom")

      Arushi sha gu'da
      "Bridegroom, experience -- ululation."

   b. Ango ba gu'da
      "Bridegroom, causes -- ululation."

   c. kirarin kuyanga ("kirari for a female slave")

      Tumun yaki manzon gu'da
      "The first harvest of war and heralder of ulula-
      tion (celebrating a victory)."

2.3. kiranye m.s.

A challenge issued on behalf of a 'dan dambe ("a
boxer") by a musician, usually with drum accompaniment, e.g., on kalangu, such challenge being in the
form of an extended kirari stating the prowess of
the sponsor/patron.

2.4. kirari m.s.

A vocal text in praise and identification of a patron (similar texts in identification of inanimate
objects and animals do not normally form part of
music performance). Acclamatory performance of
such a text may occur in isolation or at the same
time as a song or instrumental performance in honour of the same patron. A performer specializing
in the performance of kirari alone is usually known
as either 'dan ma'abba, babamba'de, marok'in baki,
mai kirari, or San K'ira, while the total performance, including the performer's motives and behaviour, is termed ma'abbanci m.s. or bamba'danci m.s.

2.5. wak'a f.s. (pl. wak'ok'i)

Any song composed by a professional or non-professional musician, or a written poem composed by a
non-professional poet. A song or poem composed on
a topic in which the singer or poet specializes may
be termed wak'e m.s., the main topics of such specialization being religion and religious teaching,
history and socially censorable behaviour. Both
the professional singer/composer and the non-professional poet may be termed mawak'i, though the
latter may be further defined as mai rubuta wak'a
m. or f.s. = mai rubutu wak'a m. or f.s. ("the
writer of a song"), or mai wallafa ("the author of
a written work"); the composition of a song may be
termed yin wak'a m.s. and of a poem, shirin wak'a
m.s., rubuta wak'a m.s. = rubutu wak'a m.s., or
wallafa wak'a m.s.; the performance of both a song
and a poem may be termed yin wak'a m.s. or rera
wak'a m.s. In addition to the above, various terms
referring to features common to more than one type
of song and/or poem are listed under 2.51, below.
Further terms referring to particular song types or
categories, are for convenience listed alphabetically under the following sections:

   2.52. wak'ar addini ("religious song")

   2.53. wak'ar bori ("possession song")

   2.54. wak'ar nasha'di ("entertainment song"), or
         a broad category including such extremes as
         tarihi ("historical narrative") and zambo
         ("songs of ridicule")

   2.55. wak'ar siyasa ("political song")

   2.56. wak'ar yabo ("praise song")

The above categories are never watertight when ex-
amined from the point of view of their texts, the
major criterion in assigning a song to one of these
categories being the singer/composer's intentions.

2.51. Miscellaneous terms common to various song-and-poem
      types.

      bege m.s.

A nostalgic longing expressed in song or poem for an absent or dead person. Such longing may be expressed in a religious song or poem (e.g., a yearning for the Prophet), a love song, or a political song (e.g., a yearning for a departed leader).

Caji m.s.

A song style thought to have been originated by Hamza Caji, and currently practiced by such singers as Hamisu Caji, Ibrahim 'Dan Mani Bauci and Dogara Caji.

'dango m.s.

A hemistich in a written poem (cf. she'dara).

fasaha f.s.

Any skill, but here applied to "literary" skill in the composition of a song or poem. The more specific term is hazik'anci (below).

gajarta m. or f.s.

The shortness of a song or poem, or of a line thereof, and as such a specific value of ma'auni.

gunguni m.s.

Humming, employed by a singer or poet in testing the suitability of a metre and/or melody for the composition of a song, or employed as a preliminary to actual performance.

hazik'anci m.s.

"Literary" skill in the composition of a song or poem (see fasaha, above), such skill being displayed in the choice of words and statements to convey an idea, and in the suitability of this choice to the metre and melody chosen for the song or poem.

lele m.s.

A positive longing expressed in a song or poem
(cf. bege, above); also the type of singing used
for tawai (rocking an infant to sleep, dandling it
on the knee, etc.).

ma'auni m.s.

The general length value of a song or poem, or of
a line thereof, the more specific values being
gajarta and tsawo.

murya f.s.

A single syllable of a song or poem, the linguistic tone or quantity thereof, or the musical pitch
or length value of such a syllable in performance.

Shata m.s.

A style of singing originated by Alhaji Muhamman
Shata, the most popular of all present-day Hausa
singers, and imitated by numerous lesser singers.

she'dara f.s. (pl. she'daru)

A written line of a poem, usually consisting of
two 'dango.

tsawo m.s.

The longness of a song or poem, or of a line
thereof, and as such a specific value of ma'auni.

wak'ar mada'ba f.s.

Literally "a song accompanying floor-pounding,"
and used as a term for songs or poems without any
structural values (e.g., no consistency of metre,
no tonal rhyming, no quantitative rhyming, etc.).

2.52. wak'ar addini f.s. (pl. wak'ok'in addini)

A religious song or poem, but most usually the
latter, of which there are numerous sub-categories
not listed here. A religious song as such is usually non-professional, though there are excep-
tions, and may be performed by almost anyone. A
particular variety exists in the many religious
texts sung for bara ("begging for alms") by crip-
ples and blind people (musaka) and Koranic students (almajirai) with various sub-categories such
as wak'ar Takutaha, = wak'ar Tukutufa (a song or
songs sung by blind women and girls from house to
house on the Prophet's naming day).

2.53. wak'ar bori f.s. (pl. wak'ok'in bori)

A song in honour or praise of an iska ("a spirit
or god"), and normally performed by musicians specializing therein either as part of an entertain-
ment/spectacle, or to invoke the possession of a
'dan bori or 'yar bori (male or female possession-
dancer) by the iska invoked. Each iska being traditionally honoured in this way with various
songs, it follows that there are various sub-categories each related to the identity of one or the
other of the numerous spirits invoked, e.g.,
wak'ar Sarkin Maka'da, wak'ar Barahaza, wak'ar
Sarkin Rafi, wak'ar Kure, etc.

2.54. wak'ar nasha'di f.s. (pl. wak'ok'in nasha'di)
= wak'ar nisha'di f.s.

An entertainment song, though this, as might be
expected, belongs to an extremely large category.
It is probably best divided into professional and
non-professional song, though even here there is
considerable overlap in subject matter.

2.541. Terms common to professional and non-professional
wak'ok'in nasha'di.

gamtsi m.s. = alfahasha f.s. = batsa f.s.

Offensive sexual comment which, when it dominates

a song text, may permit the latter to be termed
wak'ar gamtsi, though this may be a somewhat con-
trived term. Of frequent occurrence in many professional entertainment songs (e.g., gambara), it
is also found in non-professional songs by women
(e.g., work songs) as well as in songs by young
girls and unmarried women (wak'ar 'yan mata).

zambo m.s. = yanke m.s.

Satire or ridicule of an individual or group of
people, or censure of his or their conduct,
which, when it dominates a song text, may permit
the whole performance to be termed zambo.

2.542. Terms referring to professional wak'ok'in nasha'di.
Of the enormous body of songs that fall under this
category, only a small proportion permit termino-
logical grouping, as below. Thus, much of the rep-
ertoire of such famous composers and singers as
Alhaji Shata, 'Dan Maraya Mai Kuntigi, Alhaji 'Dan
Alalo and others defies any more specific classification than as wak'ok'in nasha'di.

tarihi m.s.

Historical narrative, not in itself of frequent
occurrence, but greatly esteemed by certain sections of the community and the specialty of individual singers (e.g., Sarkin Kotso 'Dan Maraya of
Daura, whose tarihin Daura, or "history of Daura,"
is fairly widely known even outside the confines
of that Emirate).

gambara f.s.

An extended vocal performance, usually by two or
more 'yan gambara (m.s. 'dan gambara), in which
the conduct of individuals and particularly their
sexual behaviour is censored and made the subject
of abuse and ridicule. In the performances of
such a master of the art as Saleh Mai Gambara,
the text is for the most part delivered in a recitation metrically regulated by the accompanying
drumming, song (in the Western sense of stable
pitch and length values) being reserved for

points of structural and dramatic importance to the performance as a whole.

wak'ar bojo f.s.

An older and now rare form of bawdy song accompanied on kukuma and k'warya.

wak'ar caca f.s.

A song about gambling which, with wak'ar shan giya below, belongs to a possibly extensive group of songs deriding human frailties.

wak'ar gwauro f.s. = wak'ar gidan gwauro f.s.

A song ridiculing the life of a bachelor or spinster, and customarily sung with or without instrumental accompaniment during Ramadan. It is, however, of more frequent occurrence as a nonprofessional song type.

wak'ar shan giya f.s.

A drinking song which, like wak'ar caca above, derides human frailty or turns up a nose at accepted codes of behaviour. Outstanding examples of both of the above apparently opposed attitudes to drinking are found, for instance, in the two songs "Sha Ruwanka Ka Hole" and "A Sha Ruwa," both by Alhaji Muhamman Shata.

'yankamanci m.s.

A mildly satirical type of performance by one or more 'yan kama (m.s. 'dan kama) compounded of song, recitation, acting and clowning; the vocal parts of the performance are frequently parodies of famous songs by composers and singers such as Naramba'da, Jan Ki'di and Sarkin Tabshin Katsina Alhaji Mamman, the major distinction between 'yankamanci and gambara being in the completely proper nature of everything said and done in the former.

2.543. Terms referring to non-professional wak'ok'in nasha'di. These are presented under categories defined by the age-group and sex of the performers.

2.5431. wak'ar yara f.s.

A children's song.

wak'ar tatsuniya f.s.

A song occurring as part of a tatsuniya, or "traditional children's story," such tatsuniya being normally told in the evenings and based on the adventures of both humans as well as animals and insects (e.g., Zaki, "Lion"; Giwa, "Elephant"; Gizo, "Spider," etc.). While such songs are normally unaccompanied by the children listening to the story, or by the narrator, more elaborate performances occur in which drums (e.g., kalangu) are used to supply an accompaniment to the whole.

2.5432. wak'ar samari f.s.

Young men's song.

wak'ar abayyana f.s.

A song in ridicule of social misconduct, and performed in connection with rawan Gane, with drum accompaniment on gangar noma, kwairama and kazagi. An example of such a song:

Mai satan rogo rani ya yi a dube shi
"The cassava thief! It is harvest time, so let's look out for him!"

wak'ar macukule f.s.

A game-song performed in the streets during the evenings of the month of Ramadan.

wak'ar rawan Gane f.s. = wak'ar rawan takai f.s.

A song associated with the dance known as rawan takai.

wak'ar tashi wali f.s.

A game-song performed in the streets during the evenings of the month of Ramadan.

wak'ar 'yan dako f.s. = wak'ar 'yan kura f.s.

A song sung by market porters pushing heavily laden trollies in and around urban markets, the singing helping to coordinate their efforts.

2.5433. wak'ar 'yan mata f.s.

A girls' and young unmarried women's song. For occasions see buki, aure, rawan 'yan mata, wasan misisi, kai gara, tashen azumi.

ga'da f.s.

A more or less spontaneous breaking into song, dancing and handclapping. The girls sing and clap while playing the ga'da game, in which they form a circle and each in turn falls backward into the arms of her partners.

wak'ar arauye nanaye f.s.
= wak'ar nanaye f.s. = wak'ar asauwara f.s.

A song with no fixed topic, but characterized by the amshi ("refrain"), which employs the apparently meaningless formula arauye nanaye, or variants thereof (e.g., aye iye ayeraye, etc.). The attempt to relate these apparently nonsensical syllables to the names of the daughters of Satan is questionable as an historical and linguistic exercise, but acceptable as an expression of the disapproval of this type of singing held by many malamai ("religious scholars and teachers"). Though such songs are performed on a variety of occasions, the accompaniment is most frequently supplied on such drums as

kalangu (with 'dan kar'bi and kuntuku , duma or
dundufa. Exceptionally such songs may be performed by wanzamai (barbers). They are most often performed on the occasion of rawan 'yan mata
and corn grinding (nik'a, see wak'ar mata, below).

wak'ar gwatso f.s.

A bawdy song sung to the accompaniment of such
drums as kwairama with kazagi or kalangu with
'dan kar'bi and kuntuku.

2.5434. wak'ar mata f.s.

A women's song. The occasions on which women
sing are varied, comprising work situations such
as daka ("pounding," with the more specialized
lugude and samammance), nik'a ("grinding," with
the more specialized marka'de) and da'be ("flattening and finishing an earthen floor"), as well
as such festive occasions as aure ("marriage"),
suna ("naming-ceremony"), and the major Feast
Days of Babbar Salla and K'aramar Salla. Accompaniment to such singing may be supplied by
ta'bi (handclapping), or a shantu or ki'dan
ruwa. While there would appear to be no fixed
set of topics for such songs, those listed below
as song types are some of the more common.

wak'ar kishiya f.s.

A song about a co-wife, and frequently a vehicle
for zambo.

wak'ar miji f.s.

A song about a husband, either flattering or
critical (zambo).

wak'ar uwar miji f.s.

A song about a mother-in-law, either flattering
or critical (zambo).

2.55. wak'ar siyasa f.s.

Strictly speaking, a song propagandizing for a political party, sung prior to the collapse of the
political system after the first military coup of
January, 1966. As such, they were of most frequent occurrence in periods preceding an election,
whether Regional or Federal, with certain musicians, especially masu goge and masu kukuma, a-
ligning themselves with one or the other of the
two major political parties in the Northern Re-
gion, as it then was. The most celebrated of such
musicians were: Audu Yaron Goge, at first a supporter of N.E.P.U. (The Northern Elements Progressive Union) before finally changing his support to
the N.P.C. (Northern Peoples Congress); Garba
Liyo, like Audu Yaron Goge a performer on goge but
always a staunch supporter of the N.P.C.; Ibrahim
Na Habu, famous as a singer with kukuma accompaniment and supporter of the N.P.C.; Ali 'Dan Saraki,
a singer and performer on kukuma and supporter of
N.P.C.; and 'Dan Maraya Mai Kuntigi, famous for
his songs with kuntigi accompaniment, and for some
time a supporter of N.E.P.U. By an extension of
meaning the term wak'ar siyasa may now be taken to
include any song in praise of a governmental authority other than those of the traditional Emirate.

wak'ar Gwamnati f.s.

A song in praise of the present military government of Nigeria and its leaders, headed by Major-
General Yakubu Gawon.

wak'ar N.E.P.U. f.s.

A song in praise of N.E.P.U. and its leaders, and
in condemnation of its political rivals.

wak'ar N.P.C. f.s.

A song in praise of the N.P.C. and its leaders,
headed by the late Sardauna of Sokoto, and in condemnation of its political rivals.

wak'ar soja f.s.

A song in praise of the Nigerian Army and its various commanders, and in condemnation of the secessionist leaders of Biafra under their leader, Colonel Ojukwu.

2.56. wak'ar yabo f.s.

A praise-song, the subjects of such songs varying from traditional rulers (Emirs and their officials) to important commoners (e.g., wealthy merchants, owners of transport companies), though even an unimportant commoner may be occasionally made the subject of a praise-song. Praise-singers themselves may be classed as either "tied" or "freelance," depending on their degree of dependence on a single patron or their freedom to act as independent agents in establishing a series of patronages. Most "tied" singers are attached to the courts of Emirs or of their officials, though a second but increasingly less common group exists among those musicians who, through their use of a particular accompaniment instrument, are traditionally, though not necessarily, tied to certain occupational classes (e.g., masu kalangu to butchers, masu komo to hunters, masu dundufa to blacksmiths, etc.). By the nature of their status, official "tied" musicians are obliged to specialize in wak'ok'in yabo to the exclusion of almost all other types of song, and this may partially explain the outstanding quality of the compositions of such singers, now almost legendary, as Dodo Mai Tabshi, Naramba'da, and Jan Ki'di, as well as those of such equally talented singers as the late Sa'idu Faro, 'Dan K'wairo and his elder brother Kurna, and Aliyu 'Dan Dawo. Freelance musicians are, however, at liberty to compose not only praise-songs, but also entertainment and political songs, though in spite of this diversity of subject matter a song such as Alhaji Shata's "Dodo Na Sardauna," in praise of the Emir of Zaria, is certainly comparable with the best of the products of "tied" musicians.

3. Instrumental Music

3.1. bushe-bushe da ki'de-ki'de pl.

Lit. "Blowings and drummings," the term in effect covers all instrumental music with the exception of performance on tambari, i.e., all blowing of wind instruments, beating of drums, blowing or plucking of stringed instruments, and rubbing, striking or shaking of idiophones.

busa f.s. (pl. bushe-bushe)

Blowing of any wind instrument (see Aerophones).

jinjina m. or f.s.

An introductory performance on a drum, wind instrument or stringed instrument, which serves both as a "warming-up" and as a dedicatory session. A jinjina is almost always based on the instrumental realization of the language tones and quantities of a non-verbalized text dedicating the performance to God, in which case it is termed rok'wan Allah = rok'on Allah, or to an important patron by naming the latter and his qualities. An outstanding example of rok'wan Allah is that text used by the head of the kakakai (kakaki) players in Katsina every morning before leaving home:

Allah ne Sarki	"God is the King,
Mai Sama ne Sarki	The Lord of the Heavens is the King,
Allah ne	God is
da gaskiya	Always right,
Mai Sama ne	The Lord of the Heavens is
da gaskiya	Always right,
Sarkin sarauta Allah	The King of kings, God.
Allah maganin	God, the answer to
k'ak'a nika yi	Uncertainty,
Uban Giji	The Lord God
Shi ba da basira	Is the giver of wisdom,
dangana Allah	Trust in God
ta fi komi	Is the answer to all else."

juya ki'da f.s.

A change of style in a performance on a drum,
stringed instrument, or idiophone. The more specific types of change are: juyen take, a change of
take; sake bugu, a change of style on tambari; sake
hannu, a change of technique on a drum; salo-salo,
the different styles of drumming on tambari.

take m.s.

The instrumental realization of the language tones
and quantities of a normally non-verbalized text in
identificatory praise of a patron as an individual,
as a member of a class, or as an officeholder.
Such texts are usually short and frequently epithetical in content, e.g., a take for any 'dan
tauri.

> 'Dan tauri sha dadala
> "'Dan tauri, experience-cutting."

Terms for particular kinds of take may be formed by
statement of the sponsor's name or class after the
word take with a genitival suffix, thus, taken
maharba, taken 'yan tauri, etc. Sponsors of take,
either as individuals or as members of a class,
are: bamba'dawa, maharba, mahauta, mak'era,
malamai, manoma, marok'an baki, samari, sarakuna,
sharifai, wanzamai, 'yan mata, 'yan dambe, 'yan
hoto, 'yan k'odago, 'yan kokuwa and 'yan tauri.

ki'da m.s. (pl. ki'de-ki'de = ka'de-ka'de)
= ki'di m.s.

Beating a drum, bowing or plucking a lute, shaking,
striking, plucking or rubbing an idiophone.

ki'dan amada m.s.

Drumming on a calabash (k'warya) -- usually a whole
set of them (ki'dan ruwa) -- in accompaniment of a
style of singing called wak'ar amada performed at
buki for entertainment of women, usually by professional female singers called masu amada. A particularly popular subject is the ridicule of co-wives.
However, the name for this style of singing seems
to have sprung from a religious song sung by men,
Koranic students or married women, in which each

verse is terminated with the name "Amada," a reference to the Prophet Mohammed.

ki'dan bori m.s.

An instrumental performance for bori, i.e., in honour of an iska and to invoke possession by that
iska. Terms for particular bori performances may
be formed by statement of the iska's name after the
word ki'da with a genitival suffix, thus ki'dan
Sarkin Makada, ki'dan Sarkin Rafi, ki'dan Barahaza,
etc. The most usual instruments for such performances are k'warya, garaya, goge or kukuma.

ki'dan bumbum m.s.

Drumming for war on kurya.

ki'dan fada m.s.

Drumming for an Emir on gangar fada.

ki'dan kwambe m.s. = ki'dan a sha k'afa m.s.

Drumming on kwairama or kalangu in accompaniment of
a kind of whirling dance, which is at the same time
a foot-boxing contest, and of songs in praise of
youths.

ki'dan magori m.s.

Drumming to attract custom by the assistant of an
herbalist.

ki'dan maharba m.s.

A performance on komo or babbar garaya, in honour
of one or more hunters.

ki'dan mahauta m.s.

Drumming on kalangu in honour of one or more butchers, special classes of such drumming being ki'dan
fawa, to announce slaughtering and attract custom,

and ki'dan hawan k'aho, as an accompaniment to
wasan hawan k'aho.

ki'dan mak'era m.s. = ki'dan dundufa m.s.

Drumming on the set of drums known as dundufa in
honour of one or more blacksmiths.

ki'dan malamai m.s.

A performance on tandu, buta, and sometimes on such
other instruments as zunguru, molo, or garaya, in
honour of one or more religious scholars.

ki'dan manoma m.s. = ki'dan noma m.s.

Drumming on such drums as gangar noma, kwairama, or
kuru in honour of one or more farmers, a specific
class of such drumming being ki'dan gayya for
gayya, in which the take of individual farmers are
drummed.

ki'dan rawan Gane m.s. = ki'dan rawan takai m.s.

Drumming on kwairama and/or gangar noma, in combination with kazagi for the annual dances (rawan
Gane) and songs (see wak'ar abayyana, above) of the
young men during the month of Gane.

ki'dan ruwa m.s. ("drumming on water")

Drumming by women on a set of calabash drums
(k'waryar ki'dan ruwa) in the accompaniment of
song, e.g., wak'ar amada and bori dancing. The
name derives from one of the calabash drums in the
set which is inverted and floated on water in a
larger calabash or bucket, and beaten with a stick.

ki'dan wanzamai m.s.

Drumming on kalangu in honour of one or more barbers, or in accompaniment of wak'ar arauye nanaye,
or drumming on ganga to attract customers and to
accompany special songs designed to lessen a girl's
fear of tattooing (ki'dan jarfa).

ki'dan wasa da kura m.s.

Drumming on tallabe or gangar noma, with kazagi for professional conjurers of hyenas. See wasan kura, maka'dan mai wasa da kura.

ki'dan 'yan mata m.s.

Performance on such drums as kalangu, dundufa, duma, kwairama, or gangar noma in the accompaniment of young girls' singing and/or dancing, though the latter may be more specifically termed ki'dan rawan 'yan mata, some of the more popular dance rhythms in Zaria in 1964 being: asauwara, na gyartai, 'dan k'odago, gidigo, mairo dike, lalayyo, lafsuru, soso, gwaja, shatan gimi and gwatso.

ki'dan 'yan dambe m.s.

Drumming on kalangu by masu kalangu for boxers at boxing matches (dambe), in which their take are drummed and songs of praise are sung (wak'ar yabo).

ki'dan 'yan hoto m.s. = wasan 'yan hoto m.s.
= kallankuwa f.s.

Drumming on gangar noma and kazagi for performance of 'yan hoto.

ki'dan 'yan kama m.s.

Drumming by 'yan kama on gangar 'yan kama in accompaniment of their humorous speeches, songs and imitations.

ki'dan 'yan kokuwa m.s. = ki'dan kokawa m.s.

Drumming of take on kwairama by masu kwairama for wrestlers ('yan kokuwa) in accompaniment of their self-acclamation (kirari) and the wrestling itself.

ki'dan 'yan tauri m.s. = ki'dan kufegere m.s.

Drumming on talle by maka'dan 'yan tauri for the public appearance of 'yan tauri. The drummers play the take of the competitors, particularly at wasan 'yan tauri, which often leads to self-acclamation (kirari).

3.2. Miscellanea.

bugu m.s. (pl. buge-buge)

> Drumming on tambari, whether such action consists of an ensemble performance by Tambura and his assistants, or of individual strokes for the installation of certain high-ranking officials and the Emir. This term is also used occasionally for the beating of other membranophones.

ta'bi m.s.

> Handclapping, whether by women or men, though the latter is rare and used only for special effects (e.g., to indicate pleading as in Alhaji Shata's "Sha Ruwanka Ka Hole").

kin-kin-kin. . .

> Human imitation of sound made by drum.

gan-gan-gan. . .

> Human imitation of sound made by drum.

4. rawa f.s. (pl. raye-raye)

> A dance as such, dancing being yin rawa. For specific dances, see: rawan kashewa, a sha k'afa and rawan Gane in Section IV, and ga'da and ki'dan 'yan mata in this section.

Hausa Index

kalangu (cont.)
57, 58, 71, 72, 77, 78,
79, 81, 82, 92, 93,
126, 132, 134, 143,
148, 149, 150
kalangun Sarki, 24, 25, 65,
79
kalankuwa, 21, 76, 80, 85,
88, 95, 107, 108, 110,
120, 122, 124, 127, 150
kallabi, 56
kambu, 56
kango, 55, 56
k'angu, 54, 56
k'ank'ara, 56
kan tandu, 56
kanzagi, 26
kara, 56
k'aramar ganga, 18
k'aramar kalangu, 24, 25,
82
K'aramar Salla, 10, 16, 18,
36, 37, 64, 71, 80,
107, 110, 116, 117,
118, 120, 121, 122,
124, 127, 128, 130, 143
karen Gusau, 4, 70
karen marok'a, 72, 95, 107
karin magana, 3, 11, 21,
25, 27, 30, 45, 63, 73,
75, 123, 133
k'aro, 56
karuwai, 106
kasam'bara, 7, 47, 52
kaskar karen marok'a, 95
K'aura, 8, 36
kayan yaji, 57
kazagi, 6, 15, 20, 21, 26,
31, 56, 57, 58, 71, 73,
80, 81, 82, 92, 93,
143, 149, 150
kazagin amada, 9
ki'da, 147, 148
ki'di, 147
ki'dan a sha k'afa, 148
ki'dan amada, 91, 147
ki'dan bori, 117, 148
ki'dan bumbum, 148
ki'dan dundufa, 149
ki'dan daren juma'a: see
waza
ki'dan fada, 148

ki'dan fawa, 121, 125, 148
ki'dan gayya, 149
ki'dan hawan k'aho, 121,
126, 149
ki'dan jarfa, 149
ki'dan kokawa, 150
ki'dan kufegere, 150
ki'dan kwambe, 148
ki'dan magori, 148
ki'dan maharba, 148
ki'dan mahauta, 74, 111,
148
ki'dan mak'era, 149
ki'dan malamai, 12, 107,
149
ki'dan manoma, 149
ki'dan nama: see ki'dan
fawa
ki'dan noma, 149
ki'dan rawan Gane, 149
ki'dan rawan takai, 149
ki'dan rawan 'yan mata, 150
ki'dan ruwa, 117, 143, 147,
149
ki'dan wasa da kura, 150
ki'dan wanzamai, 149
ki'dan 'yan dambe, 150
ki'dan 'yan hoto, 150
ki'dan 'yan kama, 150
ki'dan 'yan kokuwa, 150
ki'dan 'yan mata, 124, 150,
151
ki'dan 'yan tauri, 150
kin-kin-kin, 151
kiranye, 118, 134
kirari
definition, 134
general reference, 3, 20,
21, 38, 51, 62, 63, 64,
73, 76, 83, 88, 95,
106, 107, 109, 110,
111, 114, 118, 119,
120, 121, 126, 128,
131, 132, 134, 150, 151
of instruments, 16, 18,
23, 29, 37, 39, 41, 43,
50, 51, 82
of people, 8, 134
kirgi, 57
kirinya, 57
k'ofa, 55, 57
k'ofar tsarkiya, 56

English-Hausa Index

AEROPHONES - see under clarinets, flutes, oboes, trumpets

BELLS, clapperless - kuge: 7-8, 25, 65, 71

   performers on - masu kuge: 8, 71, 79

CHORDOPHONES - see under lutes

CLAPPERS, plaque - ruwan gatari: 9, 93
                    ruwan patenya: 10, 93

   performers on - 'yan daji: 9

CLAPPERS, ring - zari: 12

CLAPPERS, vessel - sambani: 10

CLARINETS - damalgo: 48-49, 90, 93

   performers on - 'yan damalgo = masu busan damalgo: 49,
                           90

CLARINETS - til'boro = tilli'bo = tillik'oro = obati: 48,
           49, 52-53, 59, 60, 87

   performers on - masu busan til'boro: 87

CLARINETS, parts of:

   body - damalgo: 48
          til'boro: 52, 53, 59

   reed - belu = beli: 52, 53

   resonance chamber - k'ok'o = k'ok'uwa: 48

   thread - zare: 52, 60

DRUMS, barrel-shaped closed - duma: 15-16, 27, 54, 75, 80,
                                    143, 150
                              talle: 15

    performers on - masu duma: 16, 75

DRUMS, barrel-shaped closed - duman girke: 16, 27, 54, 75
                              duma: 16
                              dumanya: 16

    performers on - masu duman girke: 75, 109

DRUMS, cylindrical closed - dundufa = dodara = dumfa
                            = totara = tudara: 17-18, 27,
                                 30, 54, 55, 56, 57, 58,
                                 59, 81, 143, 149, 150
                            uwar gida: 17-18
                            duma: 17-18
                            magu'diya: 17-18 ـ4
                            dundufa: 17-18
                            'yar dundufa: 17·18

    performers on - 'yan dundufa = masu dundufa: 18, 30,
                              81, 107, 145

DRUMS, cylindrical closed - turu: 39

DRUMS, cylindrical double membrane - badujala: 12-13

DRUMS, cylindrical double membrane - ganga: x, 8, 18-22,
                                      30, 37, 54, 55,
                                      56, 57, 58, 59-
                                      60, 92, 132, 149

    performers on - masu ganga: 64

DRUMS, cylindrical double membrane - gangar algaita: 18,
                                      20, 27, 48, 63,
                                      75, 81

    performers on - masu gangar algaita: 75, 86, 99, 102

DRUMS, cylindrical double membrane - gangar Caji: 19, 20,
                                      25, 82, 92

DRUMS, cylindrical double membrane - gangar fada: 19, 20,
48, 49, 50, 51,
58, 63, 65, 71,
76, 133, 148

performers on - masu gangar fada: 76-77, 86, 87, 88,
89, 102

DRUMS, cylindrical double membrane - gangar noma
= baragada = fya'de:
6, 19, 20, 21,
27, 30, 54, 71,
73, 76, 81, 141,
149, 150

performers on - masu gangar noma: 21, 76, 79, 81, 84,
88, 89, 98, 102, 105, 107, 108,
110, 119, 120, 124, 128

DRUMS, cylindrical double membrane - kurya: 15-16, 18-19,
20, 21, 22, 25,
27, 31, 79, 148

performers on - masu kurya: 79

DRUMS, cylindrical double membrane - kwairama: 6, 19, 21,
27, 54, 73, 80,
81, 141, 143,
148, 149, 150

performers on - masu kwairama = maka'dan 'yan mata:
21, 73, 76, 80, 81, 108, 110, 114,
116, 121, 125, 150

DRUMS, cylindrical double membrane - tallabe = gambara:
25, 27, 30-31,
73, 80, 81, 93,
96, 150

performers on - masu tallabe: 80, 108

DRUMS, cylindrical double membrane - turu: 39

DRUMS, frame circular - bandiri: 13

DRUMS, goblet closed - zambuna: 39, 63, 81

performers on - masu zambuna: 81

DRUMS, hourglass double membrane - 'dan kar'bi: 4, 14-15,
23, 24, 25, 30, 42,
54, 56, 58, 78, 92,
124, 143

DRUMS, hourglass double membrane - jauje: 23, 24, 27-28,
54, 55, 63, 65, 77

performers on - masu jauje: 28, 72, 90, 101, 129

DRUMS, hourglass double membrane - kalangu: 4, 20, 24, 23-
26, 30, 42, 54, 55,
56, 57, 58, 59, 71,
72, 73, 75, 77, 79,
81-82, 92, 93, 126,
132, 134, 141, 143,
148, 150

performers on - masu kalangu: 25, 26, 30, 70, 73, 75,
76, 77, 81, 92, 96, 98, 102, 106,
108, 110, 114, 116, 118, 121, 122,
124, 126, 127, 128, 145, 150

DRUMS, hourglass double membrane - kalangun Caji: 63

DRUMS, hourglass double membrane - kalangun Sarki: 24, 25,
28, 65, 78-79

performers on - masu kalangun Sarki: 25, 78-79, 101

DRUMS, hourglass double membrane - k'aramar kalangu: 24,
25, 78, 82

DRUMS, hourglass double membrane - kolo: 23, 25, 28, 65,
77, 79

DRUMS, hourglass open - gangar 'yan kama: 22, 54, 56, 57,
59-60, 93, 150

performers on - 'yan kama: 22

DRUMS, hourglass open - kazagi = kanzagi: 6, 15-16, 18, 20, 21, 25, 26-27, 31, 56, 57, 58, 59-60, 63, 71, 73, 75, 80, 81, 82, 92, 93, 141, 143, 149, 150

    performers on - 'yan kazagi = masu kazagi: 27, 69, 73, 75, 80, 81, 89, 96, 110, 119, 120, 121, 124, 128

DRUMS, hourglass open - kotso: 28-29, 54, 55, 56, 57, 58, 59-60, 63, 65, 79, 132

    performers on - masu kotso: 29, 64, 74, 75, 79, 86, 99, 103

DRUMS, hourglass open - kuru: 30, 149

    performers on - masu kuru: 79

DRUMS, kettle - bandiri: 13

DRUMS, kettle - banga: 13-14, 53, 54, 56, 57, 58, 63, 65, 74, 75

    performers on - masu banga: 14, 74-75, 87, 98, 99, 129

DRUMS, kettle - kuntuku = kurkutu = kuttuku = kuntukuru: 4, 18, 25, 29-30, 55, 56, 57, 59, 75, 78, 81, 92, 143

    performers on - 'yan kuntuku = masu kuntuku: 70, 73, 78, 81-82, 114, 122, 124-125, 127

DRUMS, kettle - taushi = tabshi: 38-39, 53, 54, 55, 57, 58, 59, 60, 63, 65, 80

    performers on - masu taushi: 39, 80, 103, 129

DRUMS, kettle - talle: 31, 73, 150

    performers on - maka'dan 'yan tauri: 31, 73-74, 111, 120, 128, 150

DRUMS, kettle - tambari: ix, 31-38, 51, 53, 54, 57, 58,
59, 60, 65, 89, 98, 103, 114, 116,
121, 123, 125, 129, 132, 146, 147,
151

DRUMS, parts of:

body-shell - akushi: 33, 53
banga: 13, 53
daro: 33, 54
duma: 15, 54
furya: 17, 55
ice: 19, 28, 29, 55, 56
icen kalangu: 24
kango = kwango: 17, 19, 22, 24, 26, 28,
29, 55, 56
taushi: 38, 59

carrying strap - ma'dauki = maratayi: 14, 19, 28, 38,
57, 58

cloth body cover - murfi = mulhi = riga: 14, 19, 58

drum sticks/thongs - bulala = dorina: 33, 34, 53, 54
maka'di = gulla = hurya: 17, 19,
23, 24, 26, 27, 55, 58
'yan sanduna: 29, 59
'ya'yan kazagi: 26

hole in body-shell - ido: 17, 29, 38, 55
kafar zuba mai = k'ofar zuba mai:
14, 17, 55, 56, 57
rami: 33, 58

jingle - ceba: 20, 54

lacing holes - k'ofar tsarkiya: 28, 57

lacing needle - cinki = tsinke: 17, 54

lacing ring - awara: 13, 38, 53
kirinya = zobe: 33, 57, 60
rik'i: 17, 58

lacing thong - rici: 14, 58
tsarkiya = tsirkiya: 18, 19, 22, 24,
26, 28, 29, 33, 38, 59, 77, 84
turu: 26, 59

membrane - <u>fata</u>: 14, 15, 17, 19, 22, 38, 54, 58
<u>fatar akwiya</u>: 17, 28
<u>fatar tayin dalo</u>: 17, 22
<u>k'irgi</u>: 33, 57
<u>samfara</u>: 19, 24, 28, 58, 59
<u>tambari</u>: 18, 19

membrane lapping-ring - <u>dagarya</u>: 23, 54
<u>kambu</u>: 24, 56
<u>k'angu</u>: 29
<u>kirinya</u>: 17, 19, 24, 26, 28,
38, 56, 57
<u>k'ungu</u>: 22, 57
<u>saisaya</u>: 24, 58, 59

oil for body-shell - <u>man gya'da</u>: 17, 58

oil and spice for body-shell - <u>kayan yaji</u>: 33, 57

open end of body-shell - <u>mak'ogaro</u>: 28, 58

plug for hole in body-shell - <u>liko</u>: 14, 57
<u>marfi</u>: 33, 58
<u>toto</u>: 18, 59

seeds in body-shell - <u>'dan kawo</u>: 23, 54
<u>idon zakara</u>: 19, 55
<u>'ya'yan baba</u>: 24, 59

sewing thread for membrane - <u>tuke</u>: 24, 59

snare - <u>zaga</u> = <u>zaiga</u>: 19, 22, 27, 28, 38, 60

tension ligature - <u>k'angu</u> = <u>'dauri</u>: 24, 26, 54, 56
<u>ta'da</u>: 33, 59

wax layer on membrane - <u>dank'o</u>: 38, 54, 58
<u>nake</u> = <u>nike</u>: 14, 28, 38, 54,
58, 79

DRUMS, performance techniques - <u>hannun baya</u> = <u>taushi</u>: 20
<u>hannun gaba</u>: 20
<u>taushi</u>: 20
<u>tillo</u>: 25

FLUTES - <u>sarewa</u> = <u>sheshe</u> = <u>mabusa</u>: 52, 90

performers on - <u>masu sarewa</u> = <u>masu busan sarewa</u>: 52,
69, 90

FRICTION STICKS - sam'bara = kasam'bara = sham'bara: 7,
41, 47, 52, 70

performers on - masu kasam'bara: 70, 82, 85, 109, 117

IDIOPHONES - see under bells, clappers, friction sticks,
percussion tubes, percussion vessels, plucked
idiophones, rattles

INSTRUMENTALISTS:

drummers - maka'da = masu ki'da = masu kawo: ix, 61,
62, 66, 69, 72-82, 90

idiophonists - maka'da = masu ki'da: ix, 61, 62, 70-72

lutenists - maka'da = masu ki'da: 61, 62, 82-86

wind players - mabusa = masu busa: ix, 61, 62, 69, 76,
86-90

INSTRUMENTAL MUSIC:

all types - bushe-bushe da ki'de-ki'de: 132, 146

drums, chordophones, idiophones - ki'da: ix, 62, 147

wind instruments - busa: ix, 146

INSTRUMENTAL TEXTS - take: 8, 20, 21, 23, 34, 39, 48, 51,
63, 64, 73, 76, 78, 79, 80, 86,
87, 88-89, 89, 105, 106, 107,
108, 109, 110, 111, 116, 118,
119, 120, 121, 128, 132, 147,
149, 150

LUTES, bowed - goge: 9, 25, 41-43, 44, 45, 54, 55, 56, 57,
59, 71, 83, 84, 93, 120, 144, 148

performers on - masu goge: 42, 69, 71, 78, 83, 83-84,
85, 100, 106, 108, 109, 117, 120,
124

LUTES, bowed - kukuma: 8, 25, 44, 45, 46, 59, 71, 85, 86,
92, 106, 140, 144, 148

performers on - masu kukuma: 45, 71, 83, 85, 92, 106,
 108, 144

LUTES, plucked - garaya: 6, 7, 40-41, 44, 45, 46, 53, 54,
 54-55, 56, 57, 58, 59, 82, 83, 148,
 149

 performers on - masu garaya: 41, 70, 82-83, 84, 117

LUTES, plucked - gurmi: 44, 53, 54-55, 56, 57-58, 59, 84

 performers on - masu gurmi: 44, 84

LUTES, plucked - jita: 44

LUTES, plucked - komo = babbar garaya: 6, 41, 57, 82, 84,
 148

 performers on - masu komo: 41, 82, 84, 106, 116, 120,
 145

LUTES, plucked - kuntigi = kuntugi: 45-46, 54, 55, 59, 85-
 86, 144

 performers on - 'yan kuntigi = masu kuntigi: 46, 85,
 85-86

LUTES, plucked - molo: 6, 46-47, 53, 55, 56, 58, 59, 85,
 149

 performers on - masu molo: 47, 70, 85

LUTES, parts of:

 bow - izga = yazga = tambara: 42, 55, 59

 bridge - jaki: 42, 44, 56
 kara: 44, 56

 jingle - ceba: 40, 45, 54

 neck - gora: 45, 46, 55
 sandar gamu: 41, 58

 plectrum - farke = farko: 40, 54

potash - <u>kanwa</u>: 42, 56

resin - <u>k'aro</u>: 42, 56

resonator - <u>gwangwanin kifi</u>: 45, 55
<u>ice</u>: 46, 55
<u>k'ok'o</u>: 40, 57
<u>komo</u>: 40, 57
<u>kumbo</u> = <u>kurtu</u>: 42, 43, 57

resonator covering - <u>fata</u>: 40, 41, 43, 46, 54
<u>tantanin</u> <u>dalo</u>: 45, 59

seeds in bridge - <u>'ya'yan</u> <u>baba</u>: 44, 59

strings - <u>amale</u> = <u>giwa</u> = <u>tambari</u>: 40, 43, 46, 53, 55
<u>magu'diya</u>: 41, 43, 46, 58
<u>sha ki'di</u>: 46, 58
<u>tsagiya</u> = <u>tsarkiya</u> = <u>tsirkiya</u>: 41, 42, 43,
45, 46, 59, 83

talisman - <u>kurman</u> <u>laya</u>: 40, 57

tension wedge - <u>k'aho</u>: 42, 44, 56
<u>k'ank'ara</u>: 42, 56
<u>wuri</u>: 42, 59

tuning thongs - <u>kallabi</u>: 40, 42, 43, 46, 56

MEMBRANOPHONES - see under drums

MUSIC, professional - <u>rok'o</u> = <u>garam</u> = <u>zuga</u>: 63, 64, 72,
95, 132-133

MUSICIANS, individuals:

Audu Karen Gusau: 70
Audu Yaron Goge: 42, 144
Caji, Dogara: 136
Caji, Hamisu: 136
Caji, Hamza: 82, 91, 136
Caji, Ibrahim 'Dan Mani: 82, 136
'Dan Alalo: 139
'Dan Anace: 109, 118
'Dan Dawo, Aliyu: 145
'Dan Duna, Mai Kur'di: 86
'Dan K'wairo: 145
'Dan Maraya, <u>Sarkin</u> Kotso: 139
'Dan Maraya Mai <u>Kuntigi</u>: 86, 139, 144

Watan Azumi = Ramadan: 35, 49,
   71, 87, 90, 92-93, 107,
   126, 129, 140, 141-142
Watan Azumin Tsoffi: 35, 129
Watan Takutufa: 129
zikiri: 13

secular celebrations - aure: 16, 18, 64, 72, 95, 107,
   109, 114, 117, 127, 142,
   143
buki: 64, 70, 71, 72, 74, 76,
   78, 80, 81, 83, 84, 85,
   86, 91, 92, 94, 95, 96,
   105, 106, 107, 108, 109,
   110, 111, 113, 115-116,
   117, 122, 125, 128, 142,
   147
kalankuwa: 21, 76, 80, 85, 88,
   95, 105, 107, 108, 110,
   120-121, 122, 125, 127
Rawan Gane: 5, 6, 21, 76, 80,
   89, 92, 95, 108, 123-124,
   141, 149, 151
Rawan Takai: 170
suna: 16, 18, 64, 72, 95, 107,
   109, 117, 125, 143
Watan Wowwo: 35, 129

state celebrations and
  official occasions - daba: 74, 111, 118
gaisuwar juma'a: 64, 81, 107,
   119
hawan daushe: 34, 37, 64, 71,
   84, 94, 103, 109, 119, 121
hawan kilisa: 64, 71, 94, 108,
   119
hawan Salla: 34, 37, 64, 71,
   74, 84, 94, 103, 106, 109,
   111, 118, 119, 120, 121
na'din sarauta: 64, 74, 78,
   81, 84, 94, 95, 96, 97-98,
   106, 107, 109, 111, 123
rangadi: 109, 118, 123
sara = waza: 64, 71, 79, 87,
   88, 89, 94, 109, 129
wazan Salla: 64, 109, 121, 130
yawon Salla: 64, 72, 91, 105,
   106, 107, 109, 121, 130

PERFORMANCE, patrons of:

barbers - wanzamai: 147, 149

blacksmiths - mak'era: 18, 81, 107, 145, 147, 149

boxers - 'yan dambe: 78, 106, 109-110, 134, 147, 150

butchers - mahauta: 25, 77, 106, 145, 147, 148

clerics - malamai: 10, 12, 41, 70, 70-71, 74, 107, 142, 147, 149

district heads - hakimai: 63, 64

emirs - sarakuna: 63, 64

farmers - manoma: 21, 76, 105, 107, 147, 149

girls - 'yan mata: 21, 73, 77, 80, 110, 147, 150

harlots - karuwai: 72, 82, 83, 85, 85-86, 96, 106

hunters - maharba: 41, 82-83, 84, 106, 116, 144, 147, 148

men immune to harm from metal and other hard objects - 'yan tauri: 31, 73-74, 93, 111, 128, 145, 150

merchants - attajirai: 85, 91-92, 93, 105

musicians - marok'a: 72, 107

officials - sarakuna: 10, 20, 63-64, 75, 85, 91, 93, 105, 109, 147

political parties - N.P.C. and N.E.P.U.: 108

possession dancers - 'yan bori: 70, 83, 93, 109, 117, 138

sherifs - sharifai: 147

strongarm conjurers - 'yan hoto: 21, 73, 76, 93, 110, 119, 120, 127, 128, 147, 150

wrestlers - 'yan kokuwa: 44, 84, 110, 147, 150

wrestlers with hyenas - masu wasa da kura: 21, 73, 76, 108

youths - samari: 21, 73, 77, 80, 108, 147

PLUCKED IDIOPHONES - <u>agidigo</u> = <u>jita</u>: 4, 25, 70

   performers on - <u>karen</u> Gusau: 4, 70

PLUCKED IDIOPHONES - <u>bambaro</u>: 4-5

RATTLES, pendant - <u>caccakai</u> = <u>akacau</u> = <u>akayau</u> = <u>k'oroso</u>: 5

RATTLES, stick - <u>kacikaura</u> = <u>kacakaura</u> = <u>kacaura</u> = <u>cakaura</u>
                = <u>lalajo</u>: 7, 97

   performers on - <u>'yan</u> <u>kacikaura</u>: 97

RATTLES, vessel - <u>acikoko</u>: 4

RATTLES, vessel - <u>barancaki</u> = <u>barankaci</u>: 5

RATTLES, vessel - <u>cakansami</u> = <u>cikansami</u>: 6, 124

RATTLES, vessel - <u>caki</u> = <u>buta</u> = <u>duma</u> = <u>galura</u> = <u>garura</u>
                = <u>gora</u> = <u>gyan'dama</u>: 5-6, 41, 47, 54, 55,
                   63, 70, 96, 97, 149

   performers on - <u>masu</u> <u>gora</u>: 70, 82, 85, 109, 117
               <u>masu</u> <u>ki'dan</u> <u>buta</u>: 107
               <u>'yan</u> <u>garura</u>: 96

TRUMPETS, metal - <u>kakaki</u>: 8, 20, 35, 48, 49, 50, 50-52,
              55, 56, 58, 59, 63, 65, 89, 100,
              132, 146

   performers on - <u>masu</u> <u>kakaki</u>: 51, 64, 76, 86, 87-88,
                 89-90, 101

TRUMPETS, natural - <u>bututu</u>: 48

TRUMPETS, animal horn - <u>k'aho</u>: 20, 49, 50, 51, 57, 58, 59,
                 65, 88, 89, 100

   performers on - <u>masu</u> <u>k'aho</u>: 50, 76, 87, 88-89, 89

TRUMPETS, wooden - <u>farai</u>: 20, 48, 50, 51, 54, 55, 57, 58, 59, 65, 87, 132

    performers on - <u>masu farai</u>: 49, 76, 86, 87, 88, 89, 99, 100

TRUMPETS, parts of:

    bell-end - <u>home</u>: 51, 55
            <u>turmi</u>: 49, 50, 59
            <u>uwa</u>: 51, 59

    body - <u>gora</u>: 49, 55

    bore - <u>rami</u>: 49, 58

    carrying bag - <u>jaka</u>: 51, 56

    carrying strap - <u>maratayi</u>: 49, 50, 58

    embouchure - <u>k'ofa</u>: 49, 50, 57
               <u>magu'diya</u>: 51, 58

    mouthpiece - <u>falami</u> = <u>fallami</u>: 49, 54
              <u>kara</u>: 51, 56
              <u>'ya</u>: 51

VOCALISTS, acclamators - <u>marok'an baki</u>: 61, 63, 70, 73, 76, 78, 82, 83, 89, 94-95, 96, 99, 110, 114, 116, 117, 118, 119, 120, 121, 122, 126, 128, 134, 147
                         <u>bamba'dawa</u>: 63, 76, 89, 94-95, 99, 134, 147
                         <u>karen marok'a</u>: 72, 95, 107
                         <u>kaskan karen marok'a</u>: 63, 95
                         <u>masu kirari</u> = <u>San K'ira</u> = = <u>'yan k'ira</u>: 63, 95, 134
                         <u>mawak'an bodo</u>: 95
                         <u>'yan agalanda</u>: 63, 95, 96, 118

VOCALISTS, chorus - <u>masu amshi</u>: 66, 71, 73, 74, 75, 76, 79, 80, 81, 82, 132

VOCALISTS, singers - <u>mawak'a</u>: 61, 66-67, 71, 74, 76, 79, 80, 91-94, 132, 135
                    <u>karen Gusau</u>: 4, 74
                    <u>mawak'an Amada</u>: 71, 91, 115, 147

mawak'an bege: 91
mawak'an Caji: 25, 67, 81, 82, 86,
    91-92, 105, 120
mawak'an Hamisu: 92
mawak'an kukuma: 45, 92
mawak'an Shata: 92
mawak'an 'yan mata: 92, 127
zabiyoyi: 67, 91, 94, 120

VOCALISTS, talkers/singers - 'yan magana: 61, 96-97
                             masu wasa da kura: 31, 80, 81
                             na uwale: 31, 80, 93
                             'yan daji: 9, 93
                             'yan gambara: 25, 31, 72, 78,
                                 80, 81, 93, 96, 139
                             'yan garura: 6, 74, 93, 96-
                                 97, 100, 108
                             'yan jarfa: 31
                             'yan kacikaura: 7, 96-97
                             'yan kama: 22, 93, 140, 150
                             'yan kashin kasuwa: 81
                             'yan tagaba: 82
                             'yan tandu: 11, 72, 93

VOCALISTS, ululators - magu'da: 62, 134

VOCAL MUSIC, acclamatory/epithetical
                 texts - kirari: 8, 20, 22,
                         29, 37-38, 39,
                         41, 43, 50, 51-
                         52, 62-63, 64,
                         65, 76, 80, 82,
                         83, 88, 95, 106,
                         107, 109, 110,
                         111, 114, 118,
                         119, 120, 121,
                         126, 128, 132,
                         134, 150

VOCAL MUSIC, challenges - kiranye: 131, 134

VOCAL MUSIC, proclamations - gangami: 131, 133-134

VOCAL MUSIC:

    song - wak'a: ix, 62, 67, 91, 131, 135

bawdy songs - wak'ar bojo: 140
wak'ar gamtsi: 72, 93, 96, 139
wak'ar gwatso: 143

songs of censure - gambara: 72, 139-140, 140
wak'ar abayyana: 80, 92, 124, 141,
149

entertainment songs - wak'ar nasha'di: 4, 41, 42, 46,
52, 70, 80, 83, 85, 86, 91,
92, 133, 135, 138, 139

girls' songs - wak'ar 'yan mata: 78, 110, 139, 142

historical songs - tarihi: 135, 139

songs of longing - lele: 137

nostalgic songs - bege: 85, 91, 135-136

political songs - wak'ar siyasa: 4, 42, 46, 70, 83,
85, 91, 135, 144

possession songs - wak'ar bori: 9, 41, 42, 52, 82, 83,
135, 138

praise songs - wak'ar yabo: 41, 42, 46, 74, 76, 76-77,
79, 80, 81, 83, 84, 85, 85-86, 86,
91, 91-92, 132, 135, 145, 150

religious songs - wak'ar addini: 135, 138
wak'ar Amada: 147, 149

songs of ridicule - wak'ar kishiya: 9, 11, 91, 143
'yankamanci: 140
zambo: 11, 72, 96, 135, 139, 143

VOCAL MUSIC, ululation - gu'da: 62, 67, 131, 134

Figure 1.   *Marok'a* of Zaria city drumming on *kalangu/'dan kar'bi* (left) and *kuntuku* (right.)

Figure 2.   The head of the musicians at the court of the Emir of Zaria blowing the *k'aho*.

Figure 3.   Musicians at the court of a district head in Zaria blowing *algaitai* for the Thursday night *sara.*

Figure 4.   Drumming on calabashes (*k'warya*) for *bori* dancing.

Figure 5. Rhythmic pounding of foodstuffs (*lugude*).

Figure 6. Malan Ahmadu, a famous *'dan kama* living in Zaria city.

Figure 6. Malan Ahmadu, a famous *'dan kama* living in Zaria city.

Figure 7. The chief of the drummers for farmers in the emirate of Zaria drumming on the *gangan noma* (right), and his son drumming on the *kazagi* (left).

Figure 8. *Mai komo* accompanying his song of praise on the *komo* or *babbar garaya*. Hunters are the traditional patrons of such performers.

Figure 9. *'Yan dundufa* drumming on *dundufa* and *'yar dundufa* (right) and *kuntuku* (left) in honor of a blacksmith, their traditional patron.

Figure 10. The Chief Trumpeter on *kakaki* for the Emir of Zaria.

Figure 11.   *Alhaji* Muhamman Shata.

Figure 12.   *Sarkin Tabshi Alhaji* Mamman.

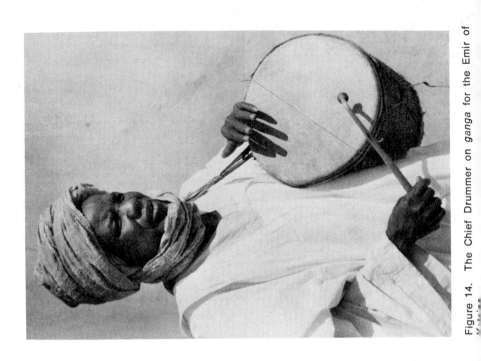

Figure 14. The Chief Drummer on *ganga* for the Emir of Katsina.

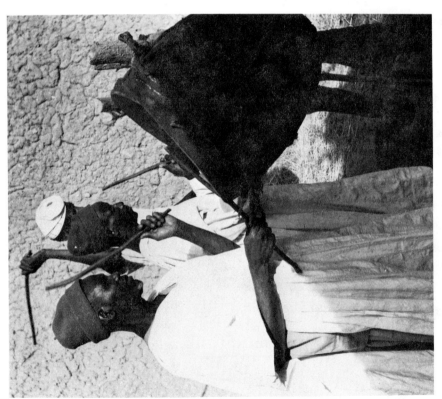

Figure 13. The royal *tambura* at the Court of Katsina.

Figure 16. Drummers on *kotso* at the Court of Katsina.

Figure 15. A *kukuma* player in Katsina.

Figure 17. The head of the *banga* drummers at the Court of Katsina.

Figure 18. The head of the *farai* players at the Court of Katsina.